How to Unlock Your Subconscious Mind

Through the Science of Mental Analysis

By
Elsie Lincoln Benedict
and Ralph Paine Benedict

Disclaimer and Terms of Use:

The Author and Publisher have strived to be as accurate and
complete as possible in the creation of this book,
notwithstanding the fact that he/she does not warrant or
represent at any time that the contents within are accurate due
to the rapidly changing nature of the Internet. While all attempts
have been made to verify information provided in this
publication, the Author and Publisher assume no responsibility
for errors, omissions, or contrary interpretation of the subject
matter herein. Any perceived slights of specific persons, peoples,
or organizations are unintentional. Always consult a medical
professional. This book is a product of its time and is not
presented to be current medical information nor medical advice.

Table of Contents

Dedicated to Our Students

By Elsie Lincoln Benedict and Ralph Paine Benedict

Profound Truths Plainly Told

Do you recall the slightly baffled sensation you experienced when a physician to whom you had gone in time of need handed you a prescription?

You took the "scrap of paper" because there was nothing else to do, and on your way to the drug store scanned it interestedly trying to decipher its meaning and especially to figure out what bearing these mysterious hieroglyphics could have on your very real and very personal problem.

But you decided, about the time you found the prescription clerk, 't were a vain ambition for a mere average man to aspire to understand the cryptic scientific code, bandied so nonchalantly between these wise technicians. You confessed it quite over your head, paid the bill and tried to forget it.

Could you have stepped behind the counter and heard the drug clerk translating your prescription to himself it would have amused you to see to what agony scientist No. I had gone to put into Latin for scientist No. 2 the simple directions for concocting for you a simple remedy which in plain United States was simple peppermint or castor oil.

The scientists in this case are going on the ancient theory that they would lose your respect and incidentally your money if they came down off their Minerva-like pedestals and told you the everyday contents of this bottle. Moreover, you might be able to make your own medicine next time, apply your own remedy — and THEN where would they be!

Medical science has contributed much to the health and happiness of man, but it could have helped much more and many more had it been placed within the reach of the everyday man as it might easily have been!

Now comes a new human science called Psychoanalysis — a science destined to do for mankind far greater things than medical science has ever done; to cure not only the mind, which the physician overlooks, but physical ailments the physician has never been able to reach.

It is not an intricate science. It deals, as do all sciences, with the simple though stupendous facts of everyday life. It can be used by every individual who once secures an understanding of it, and help him in the solution of his most pressing, personal problems.

But practically everything that has been given out to date has been, like the prescription, couched in mysterious phraseology, and written by scientists to other scientists over the heads of the everyday man whose sufferings they purport to relieve.

Musicians will play the ultra-classical, though it put the audience to snoring in eight minutes, and scorn the simple things everybody longs for; because they play not for the people but for their critical contemporaries.

Singers sing to their contemporaries, learned men talk to the learned, scientific writers write for other scientific writers — all out of fear.

Between and around these few are the unlearned, the unmusical, the unscientific — that backbone of the nation, Mr. and Mrs. Everyday American and their children.

They are in trouble. Worry, fear, poverty, grief, sorrow, disappointments and disillusionments overwhelm them.

When the struggle becomes acute the most intelligent go to books for help. Among other things they read reams on this new and wonderful psychoanalysis. It is about as understandable as the prescription. The reader, like the patient, seeks, struggles, pays the bill and tries to forget.

But he can't forget because the problem is still unsolved, not because psychoanalysis could not have solved it, but because he found nothing understandable to apply to his own troubles.

Here is a course, putting into plain, simple American terms the scientific truths recently discovered about the subconscious mind, with definite, specific explanations of exactly what it is, how it works, where it comes from, where and how it so vitally affects your life; plus definite specific instructions for applying this knowledge to your own personal affairs — in short, a prescription in English.

It is so plain you can make your own medicine next time, and after a while perhaps avoid the necessity for remedies altogether.

There is nothing in this course a child can fail to understand, yet every word is scientifically accurate and deals with the greatest problems of human life.

After all, nothing in the world need be made mysterious. Nature is performing miracles all the time, but she speaks a simple language. All the greatest facts of life can be stated in clear, helpful terms and made to do something worthwhile. Therefore, to begin with, the name of this course which includes all the significant and thoroughly tested elements of psychoanalysis and also those of everyday human psychology is translated into plain American Mental Analysis.

Clues to Our Intimate Mysteries

Here are a few of the hundreds of questions about ourselves which are answered in this pleasurable, practical course:

Why are we so different in our dreams from the person we are in real life?

How does unhappiness produce disease and why do joy and success cure it?

Why do the rich, the powerful, the beloved and beautiful commit suicide?

Why do criminals always go back to the scene of the crime?

Why does falling in love improve your mental, physical and spiritual health?

Why do we sometimes hate the one we most love?

Why does a wife call her husband "just a big boy" when he also thinks of her as" a mere child?"

What is the true explanation of love at first sight?

Why do we get over our wildest love affairs while tamer ones last through the years?

Why do lovers often feel sure they have met and mated in a previous existence?

Why do we take instantaneous and intense dislikes to people?

Why do boys fall in love with older women and girls have violent loves for mature men?

And how does this reconcile itself to the fact that women dislike to marry men younger than themselves while the older the man the younger he wants his wife to be?

Why do you change certain details when relating a dream?

Why are we afraid of certain things and why do we avoid certain others without knowing why?

Why do we often become angry, morose, elated or excited over trifles?

Why do we forget the names of people we know perfectly well, misspeak ourselves and say things we don't mean before we realize it?

Why are we poor when we want money so badly?

What is the secret of every person's supreme subconscious wish?

By Elsie Lincoln Benedict and Ralph Paine Benedict

Epigraph

I'm daily looking for a man
As on my way I go -
His features and his general plan
I greatly wish to know.

He is that MAN INSIDE 0' ME
That holds the most of good
I hat I myself some day might be,
If I but understood.

— John Kendrick Bangs

By Elsie Lincoln Benedict and Ralph Paine Benedict

Your Secret, Subconscious Self

From the deck of a steamer you see an iceberg. Always afterward you think of it as consisting of just what you saw — no more and no less. You describe its outlines to your friends and explain its size and shape as being what was visible to your eye.

Yet you saw but one-tenth of that iceberg. The other nine-tenths were floating beneath the surface, entirely out of sight.

If you have never seen a big iceberg, drop a miniature one into your glass next time you are at table, and the same thing on a smaller scale will happen.

Your Two Minds

Your mind is like that iceberg. It has its upper and nether parts — the conscious and subconscious. The conscious may be likened to the tenth of the iceberg which is discernible above the surface, for its operations and processes are always apparent to you. It consists of the thoughts you think from moment to moment in your waking hours, but lose when you fall asleep.

This conscious mind is busy handling the experiences which arise in your environment — the " awareness' ' of your surroundings, sensations of what you are doing, seeing, tasting, touching, smelling. All plans, visualizations and imaginings which catch and hold your attention are also a part of this surface mind.

You express this conscious mind more or less externally and can readily detect its operations. You can open the door on it any instant and catch it at work. Right now, for instance, you can watch your mind thinking of this page and what you are reading. You can look on while it reasons, judges and decides about what is printed here. In short, this conscious element of your mind is the mind we are all familiar with, the mind we have always known we possessed, the mind dealt with in academic psychology, the mind that does our *conscious thinking*.

The Submerged Nine-Tenths

But recent discoveries have shown that this surface mind, which we had supposed comprised all our mental processes, is less than one-tenth of the total human consciousness.

These discoveries reveal that underneath this conscious mind, part and parcel of it, bound up and wound around it, powerfully influencing it but *out of sight* are the "submerged nine- tenths" called the subconscious.

What Is The Subconscious?

This subconscious is the warehouse in which you have been unconsciously and involuntarily storing away all the impressions, memories, feelings, accumulated force and "aftermaths" of *everything that has ever happened to you.*

This means not only all the things you are conscious of having experienced but millions of sensations you were unaware of at the time. All have stowed themselves away down there in the pigeonhole of that submerged nine- tenths of your consciousness, *to be heard from later in life.*

Many of the mysteries about yourself which have baffled, discouraged or inspired you are solved by the new science of Mental Analysis, which explains this secret self that lies deeply buried but always active within each of us.

Retail and Wholesale Thinking

The conscious mind may be called the "retailer mind." It is compelled to deal with non-essentials, the externals of your hourly experiences, the thousands of details that arise in your immediate environment.

But your subconscious mind knows nothing of these. All its power is directed toward the attainment of your deepest desires. It is a wholesaler and does things only in the by- and-large.

It is not so much concerned with what you are doing, saying or experiencing at this moment, as with the massed result of the experiences through which you have already passed, plus the probable effect upon you of those you are now facing.

By Elsie Lincoln Benedict and Ralph Paine Benedict

Your subconscious mind does not so much think as feel. It does not believe or reason, as does your conscious mind. It *knows*.

Your Subconscious Ocean

Nothing you see, hear, say, think, do, feel, or experience is ever lost. Each is preserved forever in the deeps of your subconsciousness.

It is as though you lived in a houseboat on a great ocean, into whose depths something dropped every time you had a thought, a feeling or any kind of experience whatever.

Some of these are of such a nature as to throw overboard the seeds from which would grow beautiful water lilies, ferns and lacey mosses. Some would bring forth weeds, others poison ivy, while others would fringe the shore with great trees whose strength would delight you and whose shade would comfort and bless all who came that way.

Some of your deeds and desires would fling into this ocean only trash — chunks of pig iron, bits of wood, baubles, toys, debris — trappings and trimmings of idle moments, dark thoughts, primitive instincts — all would lie there at the bottom of the sea. Divers could find every one — some distorted, some washed cleaner than when they went in, but each and every one affected in some way by being there.

Many of the thoughts and things we had supposed lifeless would turn out to be fertile seeds. They would have sprouted all manner of strange, exotic, ugly and beautiful plants, each bearing fruit according to its nature and sending up to the ocean's surface the results natural to itself.

We do and say many things which are the result of the things we previously submerged in this subconscious sea.

The Stranger in Your Skin

A man does things that are "foreign" to him — not what he intended. They seem to do themselves.

He means to say a certain thing, to express a certain thought and instead says something entirely different. He forgets the names

9

of people he knows perfectly well, answers "No" when he means '
'Yes,' and in a hundred ways entangles himself against his will.

He says "that was accidental," " I said that unconsciously,"' or "I wasn't myself." But none of these is really true. The fact of the matter is that all of them were done by his subconscious. They are not accidental but in accordance with the definite law that we tend constantly to express to the outer world whatever is in the back of our minds.

We also tend to forget whatever is displeasing to the ego and to remember whatever is pleasing to it.

The Actor's Story

One of the well known actors in America told us this:

"I am often asked to dinners and other social affairs with people in whom I have no interest whatever — people with whom I have nothing in common and with whom I would rather not be bothered.

"I found that almost invariably I jotted down these engagements on my calendar for the day *following* the actual date, and was always being called up afterward and reminded of my absence.

"After a while it dawned on me that my subconscious wish not to go caused me habitually but innocently to put down the wrong date and always to make the mistake for the day after so that it would be safely over before I could be reminded.

"I arrived at these conclusions because of another strange experience I was always having of putting down engagements with personal friends for the date *previous* to that in the invitation, evidently because I was subconsciously anxious to go.

"More than once I arrived at these houses a day or even two days prior to the party — as unconscious of this mistake as I was of the opposite one "

In Our Own Lives

In a lesser degree these experiences happen to all of us — as when we find it so easy to be early at any affair we wish to attend, but late to things we dislike.

By Elsie Lincoln Benedict and Ralph Paine Benedict

Memory's Treasure Vault

The subconscious has also been called "the treasure vault of memory." In it is preserved the record of everything we have ever heard, seen, read, learned.

It never forgets. Everything you ever knew you know still — whether your memory is able to dive down and bring it from the bottom of your consciousness at this moment or not.

One reason why all persons are not able to, do this now is that we have, until the last few years, been ignorant of the fact that the mind did remember, and have taken it for granted that things passed entirely out of our mental grasp — that we had " forgotten."

A clearer understanding of the subconscious

enables even the beginner to revive in consciousness many things he had imagined completely erased from memory.

The Subconscious Never Sleeps

The subconscious is always on the alert. We now know with complete certainty that it never sleeps — in fact, that it is more active when the conscious mind sleeps than during our waking hours.

We have seen proof of this many times in our own lives — as, for instance, when we can awaken without an alarm clock to catch a 4 a. m. train if we really want to take the journey.

Nurses in hospital wards full of patients sleep soundly through all manner of outcries but awaken at the whispered request of their own patients. A mother sleeps through many disturbances but rouses at the merest movement of her sick child.

The country man upon coming to the city is unable to sleep the first few nights but his subconscious soon adapts itself and he sleeps as soundly through those same noises a week later as he did out on the farm.

Bridge Between Mind and Body

"Does the mind have a body or does the body have a mind?" is a question over which the philosophers have wrangled for centuries. Today we know that both are true and that the subconscious mind, of which these ancient arguers were unaware, is the bridge between the body and the mind.

The conscious mind functions through the brain but the subconscious functions throughout the entire body — the cerebrum, the muscles, the solar plexus, the nerves — apparently through every cell in both body and brain.

That this is no far-fetched theory is shown in the fact that its first American exponent was that greatest living material scientist, Thomas A. Edison. He says, "Every cell in us thinks/ ' and has proven to his own satisfaction that nothing is dead matter but all is living energy expressing itself in various forms.

Inner Recesses and Outer Results

There have always been those who realized the influence of these submerged selves of ours and there is not a thinking human but who realizes that many things in his life, however much they may mystify others, are but the outward expression of something in his inner life.

But it requires an unusually high grade of intelligence and an unusually frank heart to acknowledge what Mental Analysis shows us so clearly today — that:

Your money,

Your possessions,

Your good luck and bad luck,

Your ill health or perfect health,

Your environment,

Your life as a whole —

are the harvests from seeds you planted in the soil of your subconscious in days gone by.

But whether you realize it or not, these things are true. You are reaping what you have sown. The results are in accordance with laws — laws that are inexorable, unchanging, and absolutely impersonal.

Your life today is the net result of your yesterdays. Your tomorrows will be the net result of those yesterdays plus the seeds you are planting today, this hour and this instant.

By Elsie Lincoln Benedict and Ralph Paine Benedict

The only way to make the tomorrows what you wish them to be is to learn what you have already planted, how to uproot the weak and cultivate the strong things that are growing in your personality, and how to plant from this hour onward only the seeds whose fruit you desire to reap in your coming years.

This course, by showing you these things, can enable you to remake your life, as it has already done for thousands of our former students.

The Secret of the Famous

All great souls have recognized and declared that they were strangely aided by something within themselves but which they did not " reason out."

Every famous composer has said, " No, I can't tell you how I thought out the music because I did not do so. It came to me. I put down what came."

Every great poet has said, " I cannot tell you how I wrote this poem because I do not know. It said itself in my mind, and I wrote it down.

Every famous orator has said, " The right thoughts never come when I am trying to write out a speech. My audience is the other half of me. The best ideas come only when I am face to face with the crowd."

Every illustrious minister has declared, " The best parts of my sermons are never written in my study but come into my mind as I stand before my congregation. "

The " flash of inspiration' ' which comes to the lawyer at the crucial moment in his trial of a case, comes not from his conscious but from his subconscious mind, as he will tell you himself.

The reason so few people achieve greatness is not that there are but few with the spark of genius in them, but the source of greatness — the subconscious mind — is clogged in all but the few. The mental machinery of most people is full of monkey wrenches and junk, the brakes are all on and the cylinders are skipping.

The average mind is as disorganized as a rag bag.

Dr. Jekyll and Mr. Hyde

Almost every individual leads a Dr. Jekyll and Mr. Hyde life, with part of his mind pulling one way and another pulling the opposite. Then he wonders why this split personality makes no more progress.

There is no mystery about it. Such a man is never able to present a solid front to the world.

A unified personality is the first requisite for success or happiness under any condition whatever.

The energies, mentality and interests of the average individual are disorganized, disrupted, chaotic, jumbled in a mixed-up heap. Few people see the ruinous effect of this splitting of the personality, and some even consider it an achievement.

A man calls himself clever when he is able to live one life outwardly and another inwardly. He is able to appear at a social affair disliking the whole thing — the guests, the interruption to his business, even the hostess — and all the while talk and act as though charmed, flattered, delighted and happy.

"Good gracious, what an insufferable bore!" he exclaims to his wife the instant they are out of earshot.

"Society compels me to lead this double life," he will say, " My business requires it, social amenities demand it."

And to an extent these are true. But we are coming to realize that insincerity of any kind, reacts back on the personality with fatal consequences.

First among these consequences is the disintegrating of the consciousness and no man can succeed whose two minds are not working in harmony.

The Penalty of Pretense

It is not easy to lead double lives, even though they be comparatively innocent ones. Concealed facts are always popping out into open sight. Slips of the tongue, glances and postures — a hundred things betray the man who would keep out of sight his real and actual self.

The subconscious is like a vast irrigation system with every muscle a tiny headgate in the great network. A man may learn to

14

watch one or two or even a dozen of these headgates in eyes, mouth, voice and manner — but they are so numerous he cannot watch them all, and from whence he least expects it there will break out the tell-tale overflow.

A Practical Personal Science

This latest of the human sciences shows us what we have been doing to ourselves, our lives, our chances in life, our loves, hopes and aspirations; how we have been unconsciously poisoning our own wells at their source; how we have administered mental narcotics to ourselves when we most needed mental stimulation; how we have built up the present from our own past into a structure in which we now live and through which our personalities function, express themselves and meet the world.

It shows how we may easily and immediately reverse the process and begin to get the things we want out of life.

It is an essentially practical, personal science, dealing with our everyday problems in an everyday way.

Our aim and our accomplishment to date has been to give it to the student in such simple and straightforward language that it begins from the first moment to help him in the solution of his most intimate, inward affairs. It will do this for you. It will give you the insight into your own mentality which will explain to you —

Why you think and feel as you do;
Why you have gotten no farther in life;
Why some succeed and others fail.

What Are You Preparing For ?

Elbert Hubbard stated a great truth when he said," We get what we prepare for."

People bring their own unhappiness. That they do so innocently, blindly, unknowingly does not help matters. "Ignorance of the law excuses no man."

The laws which rule us and our lives are divine, unalterable. He who obeys them, whether he do so consciously or unconsciously, reaps the rewards that other people call " good luck." He who

15

consciously or unconsciously violates them pays the penalties he calls his " bad luck."

The supremest effort of life, therefore, should be to learn what the laws are which rule human happiness and how they operate, that we may consciously and constantly plant the seeds for the harvests we want.

This course in Mental Analysis has made these laws so clear, concise, graphic and understandable that anyone can put them to use in the solving of his everyday problems. They bring results from the first moment of applying them, in happiness, health and success.

Skepticism and Criticism

Some may say, "These things sound impossible." It is inevitable that some would say this. Every step in human progress has been opposed at first and forced to fight its way to recognition against skepticism and criticism.

This is due to the well-known psycho-logical fact that the average individual does not think for himself, even about his own most serious problems, but gives himself ready-made and outworn excuses for his failures and flatteringly false congratulations for his success.

Such a one refuses to believe a new thing because it is new. Thinking men and women know that the human race is in the infant stage of its development; that a few hundred years from now human beings will be doing things as far beyond our present achievements as ours are beyond those of prehistoric man.

And those who have given the subject thought realize that this progress is coming, as it has already begun to come, through the one thing that has given man sovereignty over the globe — further understanding and development of his consciousness.

Man is superior to animals in proportion as his mind is superior to theirs. One man is superior to another and achieves results superior to the other's in exact proportion as his mind is in better working order, more under his control and better understood by him.

Why We Were Not Told

"If I bring my own sufferings and successes why have I not been taught this before?" others will ask.

There is but one answer. *We are never taught the things most vital to human happiness.*

Fathers and mothers are so busy getting food for their children's stomachs and clothes for their backs, they have no time or energy to investigate or explain either to themselves or to their children how the human mind controls human happiness.

The result is that parents who would not think of feeding their children's intestines canned food, feed their intellects with canned ideas — ideas so outworn, so stale and putrid that the child is forever handicapped in the race of life.

Teachers and preachers — the other two forces which train the young mind— are so harassed by the overpowering problem of making small salaries suffice for necessities that they have neither heart nor head for remoter human ones.

Favorite Fibs

Thus we grow up, knowing "a. lot of things that ain't so" — things that are easy to teach, pretty to preach, but impossible to live up to.

We are told that " virtue is its own reward" — and see the most virtuous people all around us rewarded with kicks and poverty.

We are told that "genius is the art of taking infinite pains" — only to discover that the most painstaking people are in bookkeeping cages getting $20 a week, while every genius is notoriously incapable of taking pains with anything save what he loves — even his shoe laces!

We are taught that " success comes from hard work" — but note how the day laborer gets four dollars for working his hands eight hours, while the banker makes a fortune by working his head four hours a day and playing golf the rest of the time.

The Secret of Success

The secret of success is not hard work, painstaking effort, nor even virtue — though each of these is essential to supreme happiness.

The secret of success for every human being lies in the harmonious working of his conscious and subconscious powers.

Those who have succeeded have, in every instance, consciously or unconsciously, used their minds as they were intended to be used; those who failed unconsciously violated the laws of the mind and reaped the inevitable result.

Purpose of the Subconscious

This submerged nine-tenths of the consciousness is of the utmost significance in every human life. It has unlimited capacity for good or evil, according as it is used or misused. Each individual's life is made or marred by this vast subterranean sea of urges and impulses.

This great self is infinitely strong, infinitely courageous, infinitely powerful. It exists for one purpose, and one only — to externalize you, to bring you self-expression, to secure for you an untrammelled personality, to attain for you your supreme subconscious aim.

From birth to death it strives to set you free, to enable you to be yourself, your truest, realest self; that happy successful self you were created to be; the great self you may be, can be, and shall be.

The Supreme Wish

The greatest psychological discovery of recent ages shows us that the entire personality of every human being is built around some *one deep, consuming desire* — some supreme subconscious wish.

In one individual this supreme desire is for one thing, in another for something else, depending on the type and temperament of each, but no human being lives who does not have some deep desire at the core of his heart.

Life Built Around the Wish

That every man builds his life around this supreme wish is the explanation of many of our otherwise incredible inconsistencies, strange reactions, and of the remarkable accomplishments of apparently mediocre men and women.

Many persons know what their supreme life wish is. The most successful always know, and their success is due more to this knowledge than to any other one thing.

When we say "that man knows his own mind," we are saying much more than we realize. For there are many who do not know and these many are the failures in life.

Those who only guess are the half-failures.

No Hard Work Necessary

In utilizing your subconsciousness, strenuous effort is neither necessary nor desirable.

This mind is already organized and ready to work out for you whatever you desire. It does not need urging. It is the real you. It contains all your aspirations and impulses already. It does not require encouragement any more than a river needs to be encouraged to flow to the sea.

All it needs is direction. It is keyed for action, and has been every day since you were born. It is like a race horse that has been trained for the track. Take the reins in your hand and let it work *for you.*

You have never tested the powers within your own personality because society, schools, teachers, preachers and parents are organized against every kind of spontaneous expression of the individual.

That is why it is in danger of committing suicide — this society of ours. That is why some of its members are constantly turning against it and doing damage in the form of murder and war.

We must live understandingly before we can live uprightly.

"Getting Out of Yourself"

Do not waste time and energy trying to " get out of yourself.' ' The man who tries to get out of himself before he has cleaned house is working in the wrong direction.

The person who feels impelled to get out of himself has something wrong inside which he cannot bear to look at. So he goes to the theatre, drinks, gambles, speeds, scolds, spends money and time foolishly.

But it does no good. He cannot get away from himself. The moment the excitement is over back he slumps to the old self which is worse than it was before, because it knows and he knows the wasting of time, energy, money and thought in the attempt to drown his troubles has harmed him, entangled him more deeply and pushed him farther back than ever.

The teaching, "forget yourself for the world " is a beautiful ideal — one we must more and more live up to if we hope to be truly happy. It is necessary to the progress of the world for us to lose ourselves in self-forgetful service.

But we must learn how to do it. No one takes very long steps toward it until he settles his " internal warfare."

Every Day Illustrations

Your subconscious is either backing your work or " bucking it." It will back you in anything that is in accordance with your supreme wish. You will do the amazing tasks with amazing ease once you start.

But anything which is in opposition to it will go slowly, sadly, heavily, and inefficiently.

Whatever aids and abets your supreme subconscious aim you will labor over for long hours absolutely without fatigue, but whatever takes you in the opposite direction leaves you actually physically exhausted at the end of ten minutes.

How gladly and gaily we do a task today when it furthers some particular project! How glumly and grumpily we do the very same thing tomorrow if it no longer furthers that project.

With what vim a young girl who has always disliked housework helps mother with dinner and the dishes when her young man is there to see!

How easy it is to forget the bills we owe — but how that same memory of ours does work when the other fellow owes us!

How simple to remember the addresses, the initials, and even the telephone numbers of new people we are *interested* in, and how difficult to remember even the names of those we are indifferent to! The only difference in all these cases is the difference in the way in which a subconscious wish is affected.

Why We Fail

"If it is possible for my subconscious to get for me anything I wish why have I never gotten the things I most desired?' ' is a reasonable and inevitable question. *Because you have violated the laws whereby the subconscious operates.*

You, like everything else in the universe, are a part OF, not apart FROM natural law. Your being is responsive to and built in accordance with certain divine rules, regulations and edicts. When you disobey those you suffer, when you obey them you succeed.

The First Law of the Subconscious

You must free your subconscious of the shackles with which you have all your life crippled it; you must take off the throttles with which you have been choking it; you must give the strong self of you a chance to work for you; you must take your hands off the bridle of this swift racer that champs at the bit, and let him go.

Every great, successful, big or famous person has differed from the failures wholly and solely in proportion as he *learned* there was a deep voice within him, listened to that voice, and *let it out* for all the world to hear!

Your Problem Is You

First of all get rid of the notion that people and things and life in general are "against you." Nothing can harm you but yourself and the only way you can permanently hurt yourself is by the misuse of your mentality.

Luck is not against you. Luck is what you make it. Conditions and circumstances may be adverse to you at this moment, but if so, they are the ones you have *made* by your previous thinking. Stop that kind of thinking or you will go on piling up more adverse conditions for tomorrow.

Your Invisible Self

Your subconscious may be compared to a great ocean liner. As we gaze at her across the blue ocean what do we see?

We say we see the steamer. But what we see is her upper decks, masts and fluttering flags; the waving, smiling passengers — the life and action of her.

But there is far more to that steamer than this. There is her great body — the lower regions, the steerage, the hundreds of workmen, tons of cargo, massive machinery and powerful dynamos.

The upper decks look important, but the thing that determines how far and how fast she travels, what she carries, and whether or not she ever reaches port, depend on the way the *unseen forces work down there in her hull.*

The outside of you that men see are your upper decks. People, and perhaps you yourself, imagine these are all there is to you.

But it is only a fraction. The direction in which you go, what you do with your life, how far you travel and the port at which you arrive, all depend on the workings of the subconscious mind down there in your hull.

That subconscious is not only nine-tenths of your mind but nine-tenths of *you.* It is far stronger than anything and everything else within you, utterly fearless and unafraid.

It possesses powers beyond your wildest dreams. When you put yourself in harmony with it, it will carry you surely and safely to your desired destination.

By Elsie Lincoln Benedict and Ralph Paine Benedict

Like tides on a crescent sea beach
When the moon is new and thin,
To the lonely heart strange longings
Come swelling and surging in;
Come from the mystic ocean,
Whose rim no foot has trod.
Some of us call it Longing,
But others call it God.

— William Carruth.

Lesson I
How Our Dreams Reveal Us

The Secret of Every Dream

A secret lies back of every dream and everything that happens in a dream. Though science has but recently discovered that secret this discovery is so far-reaching and fundamental :hat already it has cleared up some of the deepest mysteries of human personality, aided in the curing of all manner of physical diseases, mental disorders and heretofore inexplicable ailments.

The new insight it has given into the psychology of every human being, and especially into his deepest desires, has revolutionized the procedure of physicians, psychiatrists, psychologists and all whose work it is to help humanity straighten out its tangles.

This startling but strikingly scientific secret of the origin and meaning of dreams is that *every dream* is *the fulfillment of one or more wishes that have been thwarted in our waking life.*

Dreams Tell Desires

In other words, everything you have or do or say or experience in a dream is the expression of some desire, longing, craving, yearning or wish which has been cheated of expression or repressed during the daytime.

One look into your own dreams will prove to you that this is true. You will recall how many times you have been doing in your dreams what actuality prevented your doing; how your dreams contain so many more of the desired elements than does real life, and how much more intense are your dream experiences than those of reality.

The poor who go to bed hungry or those who are dieting against their will, dream of feasts and banquets where there are quantities of just the food they like best. The man who retires thirsty dreams of cool springs, babbling brooks, steins of beer, goblets of wine, pitchers of ice water, or whatever kind of beverage he prefers.

A young woman friend who homesteaded a "dry farm" in Montana, told us that over and over again when she was most longing for it she dreamed of finding a beautiful deep spring on her land.

An intense repressed desire of any kind ultimately expresses itself in some form in our dreams. We dream of doing things we do not countenance in our waking thoughts but we dream them because, subconsciously, we desire to do the thing or the thing it symbolizes.

In many instances the conscious mind is not aware of this desire at all or, if it is, pushes it into the background for moral, ethical or other reasons.

No one should be blamed or criticised for the evil or "immoral" things he does in dreams. The fact that he dreams of doing them proves that he does not do them in his waking life.

Any desire that is fully gratified during the daytime is satisfied. It "gets out of the system." It is only those we are prevented from " getting off our chests " in the day that we dream of at night.

Your Two Lives

You live two lives — outer and inner. The outer one consists of what you *say* and *do*, the inner of what you *think* and *wish*.

The world witnesses much of your surface life and decides from it that you are a certain kind of person. But you know, with poignant
sadness, how little any one knows of the *real you*.

You have a thousand thoughts, desires, ambitions and longings no one has ever dreamed you possessed. You have some faults too that they would be rather surprised to see. But you have beautiful ideals, sympathies for the sufferings of others, many generous impulses and big hopes of helping humanity which no one suspects and which you feel no one would understand, regardless of how hard you tried to explain them.

The Parts You Play

One of these lives is your *surface* life, the other your *submerged* life. Each has its own consciousness, its own experiences and operates in its own way.

"All the world's a stage,"' said Shakespeare, and all of us are actors and play many roles. The tenth part of your mind which controls and handles your surface life is, as stated, the conscious mind. It is at the helm during your waking hours. It directs the role you play in the many-act drama in which you appear day by day on the stage of your hourly existence.

The part you play out here on the stage of this everyday conscious life is a part that has to conform to "appearances." You say certain lines, you do certain things, you act a certain way because the exigencies of life, the amenities and the world in general demand it.

These compel you to do a great many things you do not like to do under any conditions — in your social relationships, in your work, in your business, in your duties as a citizen, parent, friend, and as a member of society.

The Surface You, accompanied by the conscious tenth of your mind, is forced to go through these parts all the time you are awake.

Psychology of Dreams

When you " lose consciousness," out comes the other nine-tenths of your mind — the Submerged You — and takes charge of the stage.

In a flash he clears away the trappings of that sordid, humdrum play called "every-day," and instantly up goes the curtain on the perfect, the ideal, the longed-for dreams of " What I Want." This is the dream and the "stuff" of which it is made.

In it all is as you desire. You are the star of the caste, the envied, the influential, the handsome, the powerful, the all-important personage around which everything else revolves. Your real self, halted, hampered and hurt during the hours of consciousness is now strong and free and favored in these hours when only subconsciousness reigns.

27

The Dream-Doings

In your dreams you are always different from the person you are during the day. Instead of being at the mercy of reality, as you are in your waking hours, you begin to play some role you want to play, to act a part you want to act, to be some person you want to be, regardless of how fantastical these desires may be.

Primitive Nature of Dreams

In the dream there are no laws, no rules, no regulations, no inhibitions. The dreamer harks back a million years, before any of these restraints came to repress and civilize the intense, instinctive self of man, to that ancient stage of human development when every creature was free to do as he pleased in just the degree that he was able to *vanquish his enemies.*

This fact explains why we fight so hard in our dreams for what we desire and why the action is so much more crude than during our waking life.

The conventional self which dominates us during the day gives way, at night, to the primitive self which brooks no opposition, knows no defeat, has no scruples, no morals, no conventionalities — nothing but desires and their doings.

We Dream in Pictures

Because the dream takes us back to the ancient stages when the keenest sense man possessed was the visual one, our dreams are mostly purely *visual* experiences.

The senses of hearing, touching, tasting and smelling, all of which figure prominently in our conscious life, are relegated to the rear in dreams because these were less acutely developed than sight in primitive man.

Only those of the keenest auditory sense or gifted in music ever hear sounds in dreams. Only those whose gustatory senses are most highly developed ever taste things in dreams. Only those with the keenest of noses ever smell anything in a dream. Next in acuteness to the sense of sight is that of touch, and this figures frequently in dreams.

But for the most part we dream in *mental pictures*. The average dream is but a series of visual images — a moving picture in which we play the leading role which exists around and through and for our personal selves.

Difficulties in Dreams

n dreams the mind places obstacles in our pathway for the joy the ego experiences in demolishing them, and this is especially true of the dreams of Americans who, more than any other people, measure a man's success by the difficulties he has overcome.

This conclusion is based in our analysis of hundreds of individuals from almost every civilized country.

The Opera Star's Story

In California we recently conversed on this subject of the ego in dreams with an operatic star whose name is famous the world over — so famous that she was at that time traveling incognito to avoid the homage of the multitude and have a few days of rest and quiet.

She told us a dream she had had the night before. Here it is in her own words:

"I was always intensely desirous of fame. Even as a child I knew I must be a great singer or life would not be worth living. I constantly pictured myself as a famous opera star — a silly performance for an unattractive little girl whose parents were as poverty-stricken as mine.

"As the eldest of a large family of children I was responsible for little brothers and sisters who were constantly getting into the kinds of troubles that demanded my attention.

"This often irritated me beyond endurance and made me more incensed than anything in the world except one. Our parents owned a small chicken farm, and when I was not having to leave my day-dreams, fairy books and personal pursuits to care for babies I was being compelled to look after the chickens — see that they were let out occasionally but kept away from the garden.

"I hated herding those chickens with all the blind hate of childhood. I felt humiliated every time I had to look after them. Was that any business for a future star to be in? I used to think to myself.

"That was twenty-five years ago.

"Last week I came to this little Inn and registered under another name without letting anyone know who I was. No one suspected. The result was that I, who have been accustomed to homage and special attentions everywhere, was treated like the Miss Average American I was supposed to be — no favors of any kind. In fact quite the opposite.

"They gave me a North room when I had specified a Southern exposure; the girl at the news stand was flippant, a bell hop was insolent, and all around I suffered from inferior service — the kind most everybody gets these days but which I have been spared for several years because wherever I went they knew who I was.

"I suppose — in fact I admit — that all this irritated me. It humiliated and exasperated me. I could not get it off my mind. Had it not been for my intense desire to have a week of complete seclusion, I would have told them who I was at once. As it was I decided I would do so as I was leaving, just in time to get even with everybody.

"I went to sleep in that humiliated frame of mind and this is what I dreamed:

"The flippant news stand girl, accompanied by the bell boy who had been insolent, came to my door and told me to come down to the back yard. They rather ordered than invited me to come. I resented it but felt I must be as dignified as possible.

"When we reached the back yard it looked exactly like that back yard we had at home twenty-five years ago.

"There was the one scrubby tree, the weeds and stones and general sordidness I remember so well as characterizing that rear lot of ours.

"These two pointed out to me a large flock of chickens running loose, and told me that though it was their task to keep them out of the garden, they were going to a concert that afternoon and I must do it in their place.

"I bitterly resented this, especially their thinking I was such a nonentity as that. But the final insult came just as they were leaving.

"'Here are the twins.' they said, handing me over two soiled, squalling, squirming babies. I did not seem able to resist nor put into words my unutterable fury at this procedure, and before I could do anything they were gone.

"I had a very interesting book and sat down to read, only to be incessantly interrupted by the babies' getting into a nearby ditch and the chickens picking at the lettuce.

"For a while I tried to carry out my orders, then decided I would show them. When they returned the chickens had eaten up all the garden and the babies were wallowing in the water, completely covered with mud — their dresses hopelessly ruined.

"They rushed in exclaiming that the concert was a great disappointment. The star had not appeared.

"Then they spied the babies and the chickens and began to scold me. I let them say just enough to get themselves in deep.

"Then I pointed to the Western sky which had by then darkened and in which the evening star was just visible.

"There they saw — blazing across the firmament and illuminating the whole world — my name in letters of flame, *millions of miles high!*

"They gasped and exclaimed: 'Why, that 's the name of the star who didn't appear this afternoon.' Whereupon I explained very modestly, ' Even a star can't be in two places simultaneously, and I was here you see.'

"Then as the horror of the thing they had done came over them and they began to apologize, I haughtily lifted my skirts away from them and their muddy babies and sailed off, leaving them utterly crushed and bitterly bewailing the fact that they had missed this chance with the world-famous star they adored!"

Explanation of Her Dream

This dream is so obvious it scarcely requires explanation. Nevertheless it is interesting to note how true to form it runs and how it illustrates almost every phase and element of dreams.

To begin with, the opera star's dream has the clarity, vividness and intensity which characterizes most of the dreams of successful people.

Any individual who is getting from everyday life so much satisfaction, fame and fortune as this illustrious woman, does not think in the double symbols which are forced upon the unsuccessful or disappointed.

Things as they are being highly gratifying to her, this woman thinks in terms of things as they are, with little subterfuge, pretense, or symbolization.

The star's ego had been wounded by the news stand girl and the bell hop, and she reasoned thus to herself, "They would treat me very differently and deferentially if they dreamed who I was." So in her dreams these two unappreciative people (whom she supposes know of and adore the person she really is and would give anything to associate with her personally) are reduced to utter humiliation, and she triumphs gloriously.

All the ignominy she permits herself to suffer tending the chickens and the twins is endured for the sole purpose of thoroughly humiliating those two people who snubbed her during the day. (You note how she didn't really tend the garden nor the babies very long, but got her revenge even before the parents returned, by letting the babies ruin their dresses and the chickens ruin the garden).

In her dream she achieved complete revenge — even to the sailing off with her skirts held away from them as she would like to do in the hotel lobby.

The babies and chicken-tending were old images stored away in her subconscious from childhood and used in this dream as symbolizing the extreme humiliation which she felt when ignored and insulted by the girl and the bell hop.

Her name, lighting up the entire sky in letters of fire, is the one mental image which above all others would symbolize fame in the mind of one who had always been ambitious. The evening star was a very obvious symbol of herself, " the star," closely connected with the famous and shining name, blazing there in the firmament for all the world to see.

This dream differs from the average dream in that it was exceedingly long, and at the same time coherent and integrated from beginning to end.

There were no missing links, no disjointed parts. The entire experience was vivid, coordinated, with every part fitting into place like a mosaic into a pattern.

"I often remember snatches of dreams," she said, " and fleeting dream-experiences that do not appear to belong anywhere, but this one was as definite and dramatic as a play, with nothing extraneous, nothing isolated. It was more clear, in fact, than almost any actual experience I ever had."

This latter fact is often true of our dreams and for two excellent reasons:

The first is that the dream is the product of the subconscious which constitutes nine- tenths of the mind and is nine times more powerful.

The second is that in dreams our attention is not diverted by irrelevant or marginal things such as distract us during waking hours, but is concentrated exclusively on the dream. You will recall how in dreams you are never interrupted by other people's taking the stage, and are never aware of any time, place or condition other than those of your dream.

Dreams and Day Events

"My dreams seem to be nothing but left-overs from the day's experiences" says many a one, and this at first glance seems to be the only tangible significance of most of our dreams.

But that there is a far deeper meaning you may see for yourself by noting that though many a dream *begins* with some event of the day, it never *sticks to the facts* of the original occurrence but branches off into other directions, injecting all manner of new details which are in themselves irrelevant.

In every instance you will note that the dream is built around a recent event which was in some way a *disappointment to you*. In the dream you go back and make changes to suit your subconscious self.

You live over certain elements of the experience, or live it over up to a certain point. From that point onward, instead of adhering to what actually happened the dream carries out what you wish had happened.

Dreams That Mystify Us

And now we come to one of the most interesting things about dreams — their symbolism.

As you have read this lesson, perhaps you have been thinking, "But how can my dreams come from my desires? Why, I have often had dreams in which I did things I didn't like and experienced all manner of things I didn't desire."

This apparently paradoxical condition delayed for many centuries science's unraveling of the real meaning of our dreams.

Then a few years ago there was discovered the most significant fact of all — that we dream not only in pictures, but that those pictures are full of symbols.

In other words, the subconscious, which is in control of our dreams, is full of symbols, each of which represents, in the mind of the individual, something very definite. This symbol stands for this definite something because of its having been connected with some experience of the individual's life (usually in his childhood) in such a way as to fasten it into his subconscious mind.

There are several reasons for this, the chief one being that the subconscious is not a reasoning but a feeling, knowing mind. It simplifies all things, reduces them to their lowest common denominator.

So when the individual passes through some especially vivid experience it is filed away in the memory — not as a detailed, minutely-recorded thing like a page of statistics, but as a highly colored picture.

In every case the picture will relate to whichever element was experienced at the moment of the highest pitch of emotion. This emotional element is what makes any experience vivid in memory.

More will be explained concerning these pictures and their far-reaching effect upon the individual's life, in the next lesson, but for the present it is sufficient to know that your mind has automatically been filing away these symbols ever since you were born and that very early in life you acquired one for almost every kind of thought, feeling or group of thoughts and sensations you experienced.

Dreams, being almost exclusively in pictures staged by the subconscious, deal in wholesale fashion with these old mental pictures of ours.

Your Mental " Morgue "

The best illustration of how the subconscious mind utilizes old symbols in the making of new dreams is seen every day in the office of big city newspapers.

Every newspaper has filed away, numbered and indexed, every picture it has printed in previous issues. This department is known fittingly, though uncannily, as "the morgue."

These pictures correspond to the pictures you unconsciously filed away in your subconscious as symbolizing your previous experiences. That your subconscious, like the newspaper office, files these away at the time and then forgets them till they are needed again, makes the analogy a perfect one.

There are thousands of these old pictures, photos, illustrations, cartoons and diagrams stowed away in the newspaper's "morgue."

The keeper of the morgue remembers only the merest fraction of them. But when a striking thing happens — when something " breaks," as the newspaper world says — the morgue is called upon for any pictures which can be utilized to illustrate the story in that day's issue.

This accounts for the fact that you sometimes see ancient photos,. with hats, coiffures and clothes that have been out of style for twenty years, used in connection with new stories.

The editor used these only for lack of newer ones. New pictures of private individuals are not easily secured by newspapers, just as new symbols are not easily acquired by your subconscious mind and, as the newspaper is compelled to use pictures (symbols) representing an individual as he appeared at some function or affair twenty or thirty years ago, so the subconscious digs up and uses in our dreams old, old symbols which stand for experiences, thoughts and emotions which we experienced many years ago.

Your conscious mind may be likened to the city editor who keeps in momentary touch with everything happening around him. Your subconscious acts and reacts precisely as does the keeper of the newspaper's picture gallery. It takes no more notice of what is passing in your immediate surroundings moment by moment than the morgue keeper takes of the news happening in the great city.

That isn't his job. But when anything exciting or interesting, and especially when something highly dramatic or sensational, happens in your everyday life, either as a desire or an actual experience, the city editor of your conscious mind reports it to the keeper of your old subconscious picture gallery and he furnishes the illustrations for the picturesque edition that floats before your mind in the form of dreams that night.

Every dream gets its original impulse from some recent personal experience or desire which hinges on something that has just previously happened or been hoped for, as does every story or article printed in the daily paper. By ten o'clock in the morning the dreams of the night before are as out of date and forgotten as is the newspaper of the day before.

The conscious mind is busy, just as is the city editor, with the problems of the present — getting ready to print a new edition.

What the dream edition prints in your mind's eye that night will depend on which of the day's experiences have most intimately and emotionally affected the ego or your subconscious wishes.

This accounts for the fact that we dream many dreams during each night, some related and some unrelated to each other. Though many people do not recall their dreams the next day no one has yet been found who, when suddenly awakened, was not in the midst of some sort of dream.

He may forget it an instant afterward, but he will have at least some slight realization on the instant of waking that he was having some kind of dream-sensation.

Dreaming What You Do Not Want

When you dream of having things or doing things you dislike or are indifferent to — that is, whenever the desire is not apparent in a dream, think back through your experiences and see if you cannot recall what the dream-pictures symbolize in the back of your mind. For the following law operates in every dream.

Law of Symbols

When a dream contains elements which of something which is deeply desired either by the conscious or subconscious mind, and usually by both.

Nightmares are merely dreams containing desires whose symbols are not pleasant ones, and in which the action, which is also symbolic, becomes so intense it awakens the conscious mind from sleep.

The Nurse's Dream

A case illustrating the use of symbols in staging subconscious wishes in dreams came under our notice several years ago.

A nurse of high standing in the city of San Francisco wished to have analyzed the following dream which had recurred until it had become an obsession:

She said, "The hospital has an insufficient staff of nurses so I am busy all day and part of the night. This has continued for many months and I am getting so worn out physically that unless I am able to free myself of the distracting dream which often awakens me with its horror I shall have to resign.

"Every time I fall asleep, if only for a moment, I have this dream:

"I am standing at the foot of a bed in the ward, where of course I have witnessed many deaths. The white screen which we always place around a cot in the last moments looms up in this dream as clearly as it does in my waking hours.

"But instead of a stranger it is one of the former hospital doctors who lies there dying. I see his agony and the death struggle, his appeal to me to save him.

"But just as I try to do something the dream ends — soon to begin all over again."

The full understanding of her dream so clarified the subconscious of this young woman that in four days it ceased to recur — a recovery much more rapid than is possible in most cases.

Her frankness, sincerity and previous scientific training, added to the fact that the dream was easily analyzed according to symbols, made the cure a simple one.

The Nurse's Dream Explained

The death-bed had become, unconsciously, a very significant symbol in the nurse's mind — the symbol of something she deeply desired.

She had, despite valiant efforts to the contrary, and despite the fact that she would not admit it to herself, fallen in love with one of the hospital physicians who was already married.

Some months prior to her coming to us this physician had resigned from the hospital board and had moved to another city. The last time she had seen him was when they officiated jointly at a death-bed scene in the ward.

She had lived this last moment with him over so vividly, had recalled the emotions with which she had been torn at the time (knowing, as she did, that he was leaving) that it became fixed in the subconscious as a symbol of his presence.

Subconsciously she had longed to have the wife's place, to minister to him, endear herself to him and be able to do something very great for him — something that would make him care.

To save man's life is the surest, quickest route into his gratitude and affection, so the subconscious devised this little drama.

When she met her situation frankly and when she realized that the dream came from her own mind and was not, as she had feared, a premonition of the impending death of the doctor, the condition cleared immediately.

The Speaker's Dream

A dream composed entirely of symbols recurred to a woman on an average of two or three nights a week for over twenty-five years. She said:

"In this dream I am laboriously climbing over huge boulders, deep ravines and tremendous crags in my efforts to reach the top of a high mountain whose sides are almost perpendicular.

"Far down below — straight down below in the bottom of the canyon — there dashes over the rocks a mad, rushing, foaming river. I am constantly on the lookout to prevent myself from falling for I know I would be mangled to death long before I reached the bottom if I should lose my footing.

"Now the strange part of this is that I am never really frightened by this great height nor actually in danger of falling, for I am wearing thick-soled, heavy mountain shoes which enable me to secure a sure and solid footing. Though I can never climb as rapidly as I desire I am always making good progress.

"Another strange thing in this dream is that I always have one boon companion — William Jennings Bryan. He walks by my side, though he never takes hold of my hand nor offers to help me. But he is extremely courteous and we chat pleasantly and in the most simple friendly way as we climb upward.

"A great many people are in our party, but Mr. Bryan and I seem to be finding the path by which they are to climb. Every little while we lean over the precipice and call down to them. They make headway and some of them climb very fast. These seem happy and exceedingly grateful to us for showing them the way and blazing the trail.

"In this dream Mr. Bryan and I are very simply clothed — he in an old fashioned suit and I in a durable brown serge. Mr. Bryan carries in his right hand exactly sixteen different kinds of flowers — columbines, brown-eyed susans and other wild flowers- while my arms seem to be loaded with those dark red blooms called 'Bleeding Hearts.'"

Explanation of the Dream

This dream, so symbolical from beginning to end, is crystal-clear when the woman's supreme subconscious wish, plus her childhood experiences, are made known.

She had grown up in the wildest part of the Rocky Mountains, and mountains became to her the symbols of "the heights" to which her ambition pointed. This ambition was to be a great orator — an orator like Bryan, whom she had first heard of when he ran for President in 1896. Mr. Bryan became to her the symbol of her oratorical ambition.

Having lived all her life in the fastnesses of the mountains this young woman's symbols all bore the marks of her early environment. This accounted for the fact that though she was a woman of middle age when she told her dream and had for many years lived exclusively in great cities, the symbols in the dream had never changed.

Neither did the dream-elements alter so much as a hair's breadth, and the reason for this too is obvious.

Her ambition, her supreme subconscious wish, had never changed. From her youth she had desired one thing above all others — to be a great speaker. And though she desired it so much that she became a well known lecturer, she still dreamed the dream because she had never reached the complete fulfillment of her ambition.

She came, in years, to have audiences which filled the largest auditoriums, but she had other ambitions than speaking to great crowds, though this element was naturally always present in her desires.

That Mr. Bryan carried sixteen kinds of flowers to one was amusingly symbolical of Bryan's first slogan, "Sixteen to One."

The most significant symbol in this dream is that of the "Bleeding Heart" flowers that "loaded down her arms."

She grew up in poverty, and her youth was black with those hardships known only to pioneer and especially mountain pioneer regions.

40

By Elsie Lincoln Benedict and Ralph Paine Benedict

At an early age she came to sympathize with all the poor and struggling because of her own struggles and poverty — and to think of their broken hearts in the terms of the "Bleeding Heart" flowers that grew on the mountains near her home.

She longed to help these others who were poor and ambitious up the heights along with herself, and wanted to do it through oratory — the simple, sincere kind Bryan used. In all her dreams, even after she came to realize this ambition in great measure, she dreamed the same thing over and over because she was still struggling, still climbing, still trying to go higher and take more people.

Sometimes their burdens seemed to load her down," as did the flowers they symbolized, but always "they made progress" and always she was confident she would not fall into the canyon symbolizing Failure because she wore mountain shoes and planted her feet solidly on the ground.

They were symbolic also of her certainty that she "stood on solid, scientific ground," that she had grounded herself in what she was teaching; that she had a good foundation for what she was doing.

Her plain brown serge symbolized the simplicity which the woman had always held as an ideal.

This dream is more pleasant than otherwise — containing just enough of the struggle element to stimulate the courage and test the ambition — so she has never tried to be rid of it, and indeed is better for having her greatest ambitions and ideals run off in this dream-movie to keep her reminded that the top has not yet been reached.

How to Unlock Your Subconscious Mind

If you can keep your head when all about you
Are losing theirs and blaming it on you;
If you can trust yourself when all men doubt you,
Yet make allowance for their doubting too;
If you can wait and not be tired of waiting,
Or, being lied about, don't deal in lies.
Or, being hated, don't give way to hating,
And yet don't act too good nor talk too wise;
If you can fill the unforgiving minute
With sixty seconds worth of distance run,
Yours is the Earth and everything that y s in it,
And — what is more — you'll be a Man, my son!

— Kipling.

Lesson II
Your Emotional Niagara

Honeymooners, tourists, and passers-by may see Niagara Falls as only a great spectacle. But to the engineer, the scientist and the man who stops to think, it is a great spectacle, plus.

He sees its mighty avalanche in the terms of power — the power that furnishes light and heat and driving energy for cities hundreds of miles in every direction — a torrent, swift, swirling and stupendous. Dashing over the precipice its gigantic force instantly annihilates everything before it, but with its energy harnessed in electricity by the mind of man it becomes a powerful constructive current.

Your Own Niagara

Within every individual there is a seething current of feelings, impulses, instincts — his emotional Niagara.

It is primal, elemental, overwhelming. If uncontrolled it will handicap, cripple or completely destroy him — according to the type and temperament of the individual.

In some types the emotions are for the most part like a wide Mississippi. Such are the unruffled people. In other and very methodical types the current is apparently measured out with the precision of an irrigation system, while in others it is a rapid mountain brook with its current never still and never put to any constructive use.

If we waste our emotional energy on non-essentials we are like the brook that babbles and bubbles without doing anything for itself and evaporates, till at the end of its life journey it is nothing but a trickle, financially and otherwise.

If, for any reason, we have little emotional energy and open the headgates only enough to do this little thing and that, in methodical routine, our conserving will do but little good.

Emotion and Success

You have seen men and women who took the same street car at the same corner at the same moment every morning for years. This is the conserving type — and it conserves everything, from food to feelings.

Such a man is never late at the office. He never misses a day, he never leaves five minutes early. But *he never goes to the top.* He lacks emotional energy — that great power which in men corresponds to horsepower, and should be called human power.

His human power is always under control, chiefly because there is so little of it. He measures it out as a New England grocer measures out sugar — two grains at a time!

These people run their lives like train schedules and are about as impersonal.

At the next desk there is a man not half so faithful, not a tenth so careful. He is late occasionally, has a day off now and then and instead of doing his work like a machine, slows down some days and races like mad others. But he is the one who gets invited to the social affairs at the boss's house and when a promotion is being passed around he is the man who gets it! He is full of human power. Half organized, he can go farther and faster and accomplish more for the heads of that business than the emotionless man.

Control Your Current

But if the emotional man forgets to control his torrent; if the powerhouse of reason is closed up so often that the force of the Niagara is not transmuted into electricity for running the main plant — his life — he can and will wind up a failure.

The most desirable human possession in the world is emotion. Without it, man is colorless, bloodless, lifeless. He can neither experience a great enthusiasm nor kindle it in others.

But it must be controlled by his mind, and its power turned into constructive channels if he would be happy and successful.

Psychology of Emotion

Emotional energy may be likened to an electrical current in other ways. It is sometimes decreased, as when we are asleep.

44

For the most part we are not made conscious of it because it is expended as fast as generated — used up in the activities of every day.

But there are other times when we are conscious of intense feeling — when something pleasant or unpleasant has happened which generated, sometimes instantaneously, an excess of this current.

Do You Repress or Express ?

Whenever this happens you do one of two things. You cannot turn the current back to nothingness. It is there. It is intensely alive. You either express it or repress it.

If you express it you are immediately relieved. This explains why the types that have the most fiery tempers forgive quickest.

They get it "out of their systems."

It also explains why those that say nothing when angry nurse their grudges. The people who tell you what they think when offended are never pernicious. Those who hide their feelings usually seek revenge later, sometimes long after you have forgotten the incident. They have "saved up," stored away their emotion, awaiting an opportunity.

Corking Your Bottles

Keep the cork out of a bottle (which is what the outspoken type is doing) and there is little danger; put the cork in and it ferments. Keep the lid off the kettle and the boiling will do no harm. But keep it on tight and there will be an explosion in some direction.

If the emotion you feel is one which cannot be expressed freely and fully in the way it craves; if for any reason you are compelled to push this violent feeling into the background, you may imagine you have short-circuited it, but Mental Analysis proves that such is not the case. You have only stored the current.

A switching of the current to something else, through which it can be fully and freely expended, is the only solution in this case.

Cause of Emotion

Every emotion is the combustion that ensues when something has happened which set fire to instinct.

Each of your instincts is a pile of tinder, laid ready for lighting, and handed down to you from remote ancestors. These bundles of tinder "catch fire" easily. They are always ready to blaze up.

Some of them flame out early in life. The instinct of assimilation burns in the new born babe. It is hungry. There is no thought behind its cry for food — nothing but blind instinct.

Other instinctive fires are lighted later on — the sex instinct at adolescence and higher ones as we proceed through life. We become more reasonable as we grow older because reason is given more and more ascendancy as the fires of instinct die down.

But all emotions are the temporary flaring up of the instinct fires. The expression "he got into a heated argument," is not an accidental phrase.

Neither is it accidental that we say he is a cold nature." Such people are never as emotional as the ones we call '" warm natures.
"

If you can imagine for a moment that though you are a human being, you are full of little banked fires called instincts which are fanned into flame by certain things, you will never again wonder why it is that you become heated literally as well as figuratively when gripped by emotion.

Two Kinds of Emotion

Emotions are of two kinds — pleasurable and painful.

When something occurs to arouse an instinct you do one of two things, as referred to above — repress or express. If you gratify the instinct, the accompanying emotion will be *pleasurable*. If you thwart it the accompanying emotion will be *painful.*

Thus, when you become hungry your instinct of assimilation is active. If, when thoroughly aroused, you can sit down to a delicious meal, the emotion is a pleasant one. But if prevented from eating the emotion generated will be a painful one.

Two Kinds of Instincts

Society, as we all know, is organized against the free and full expression of certain instincts.

Laws, rules and social customs exist for the purpose of regulating the expression of certain primitive ones which have come down to us from such remote ages that they are habitually and easily aroused; and for the rewarding of certain other and higher instincts which are so recent in us that they must needs be constantly encouraged and upheld to be kept growing.

Thus we see society praising generosity — an expression of the recent instinct of altruism — and punishing profiteering which is an expression of the remote and primitive instinct of greed.

It rewards the courageous and ostracizes the coward because his cowardice is the expression of the ancient instinct, Fear.

It teaches the young to emulate the example of the ambitious, the idealistic, the fastidious, though ambition, idealism, and fastidiousness are instincts, too. But they are high instincts and make for the *good of society* as a whole.

Society knows this and safeguards itself so far as it is able. By exacting penalties of various kinds (according to the destructiveness of the instinct involved in each case), it compels more repression of the lower and additional expression of the higher.

This is necessary and right, and will eventually lead to the elimination of the worst and a development of the best in man.

What It Does To Us

But meanwhile this does not alter the fact that present-day man, possessed as he is of powerful primitive instincts, finds it very difficult to adapt himself to civilization's code.

Something is always occurring to strike the match to an instinct and unless it happens to be one which society favors he either expresses it (in which case he risks society's penalty) , or he suppresses it (in which case he pays a personal penalty in some form, depending upon his own type and the intensity of the urge).

Neither of these is desirable. Therefore, it is imperative that the fire of every emotion be permitted to burn out, but that instead of being allowed to destroy should be put to constructive use.

Psychology of Sublimation

Suppose there is a bonfire in your back yard. If you throw water on it, it may smolder and break out later. If you allow it to go unchecked it will endanger not only your own house but the homes of your neighbors and perhaps the entire community in which you live.

There is but one thing to do. You must control that fire and give it something constructive to use its force upon.

In your house there are a number of things you have planned to cook. Bring them out, put them over the blaze and let it be doing something worthwhile with its heat-energy. Then when it has burned itself out you have done something constructive instead of destructive; you have hurt no one, accomplished something for the betterment of your own affairs and perhaps in the doing prepared extra food for the hungry. This would be sublimation.

Instincts and Individuality

The keynote of a man's nature which we sometimes speak of as his individuality is largely determined by his predominant instincts.

These instincts are outlined in the externals of that individual. Every general kind of inner impulse which is common to the human race has outer gateways through which it travels to reach the world and which are indicative of the amount and intensity of that particular urge in the individual's makeup.

Effect of Expressing Emotion

The immediate effect of completely expressing an emotion is a *feeling of satisfaction*. This is true regardless of whether the instinct is destructive or constructive, recent or remote and also regardless of the type of the individual.

But if the instinct is a destructive one and the individual a man predominantly of high instincts — that is, if he is highly evolved, idealistic or thoroughly civilized — this feeling of satisfaction will soon give way to one of regret, self-criticism or, in extreme cases, remorse.

If he is low-grade evolutionally — if he is a man most of whose instincts are primitive and remote — this feeling of satisfaction will last for a long period and the action, no matter how unsocial, may never be regretted.

If You Are a Regretter

If you are one of those who are constantly making certain kinds of mistakes and constantly being torn with regret for having made them, remember this: you are dominated too often by some primitive instinct;, but the great *majority* of your instincts are *high grade* or you would not have the regrets.

Such a man can always learn. He can adapt himself, improve himself, and if you half try you can overcome your weaknesses. But the remorse you have had, the twinges of conscience you have suffered are certain proof that you have high grade ore in you to a greater extent than the average person.

Let this fact sink in, then make up your mind not to spend any more time blaming, criticizing, despising or loathing yourself, for *these mental attitudes are fatal to work and happiness.*

You have done enough of that for a hundred lifetimes. Hereafter use all your energy self-confidently, apply it to constructive things. From this time on never waste another moment in remorse no matter what you have done.

When you make mistakes the next time don't become depressed. You can indulge in a little healthy disgust if you must, but never discouragement. Remind yourself that every person in the world who ever made anything worthwhile, made many grave errors and committed many sins.

The difference between great minds and the rest of mankind was not that the great ones did not make mistakes but that they refused to be crushed by them, got up, shook the dusk off their minds and proceeded to make up for it by doing something constructive.

You must do the same, or the future will find you more and more unhappy. Unhappiness leads to more sin, wrong and crime than anything else in the world, but happiness is a powerful aid to goodness.

The Business Man's Story

A man came under our observation several years ago whose health had become undermined. Metabolism tests proved that no specific thing was organically wrong but showed almost every organ functioning sub normally.

He had once been a man of means, with a good business, but had lost it several years before. Since that time he had gradually gone down financially, physically and mentally, till his friends could scarcely recognize in him the person they had once known.

Yet he had no bad habits, his system was organically strong and mechanically perfect. So far as could be determined there was nothing to account for his disintegration.

His home life had been ideal and his wife was devotion itself. He loved her dearly and took pleasure in the achievements of their two girls who were talented musicians.

He could shed no light on the matter, either for his physicians or for us. He ate well and slept well. But he had lost all interest in living and refrained from committing suicide only out of consideration for his family.

An analysis showed that the trouble had started during a period when he began to despise himself for having done what was, to his high sense of honor, a contemptible thing. Thousands of others would have had no more than a momentary regret, if any, but this self-loathing ate its way into his mind till it consumed him.

He had been sent as a delegate from his district to a convention, but owing to the illness of one of their daughters his wife could not accompany him.

On the train he met a very charming woman whom he had known very slightly in his youth, and who had become so successful a business woman herself that she also was a delegate to the convention.

It happened that they stopped at the same hotel and, entirely without prearrangement, ran into each other constantly during the convention. As each was there alone they ate most of their meals together and, by the time the convention neared its close, he had become decidedly though not deeply attached.

He was not a talkative man, but during their last day on the train and in response to an inexplicable impulse in the midst of a champagne supper on the diner, he told her the details of a highly dramatic but regrettable episode in the girlhood of his wife.

Her sin had never been found out, and she had atoned for it by a life of goodness and gentleness. She had confessed it to him fully and he had not only forgiven her but forgotten it now these many years.

An hour after his arrival home he would have given ten thousand dollars to have the story back. At first he lived in the fear that the woman might relate the story, but when her death a month afterward precluded this his regret at having told her was not lessened.

In his own estimation, his conduct had been all the more unpardonable and unforgettable because he was by nature a man of extreme reticence and unusual refinement. His regret became remorse. He could not look at his wife nor hear her voice on the telephone without being reminded of what he had done.

The incident repeated itself in his mind all day and in his dreams all night. He considered himself beneath contempt. He grew to despise himself. He secretly called himself "rotten to the core" and, as he expressed it, "a man without character, devoid of all manhood."

This so wore on him that nothing seemed of any importance in comparison. He had always prided himself on his character and now felt he had none. The result was inevitable to one of his sensitive temperament.

He soon began to lose his grip on business. This made it increasingly difficult for him to give his wife and daughters the things they desired and this in turn increased the self-contempt which was causing the trouble.

Being a business man and a rather ultra-practical one at that, he had never conceived of the idea that his mental condition was in any way responsible for his physical and financial ones. But he at last sought advice.

When told that the strange situation could have had none other than a mental foundation he recalled the sufferings just related.

Upon being shown that his remorse, which had become a prolonged, painful emotion, was not only the cause of his disintegration but the proof that he was by nature a man of the highest impulses, he began to get well, and is today a bigger, better business man than he was before.

The Stenographer's Story

To be forced to do things calling for extreme development of some instinct which in that individual is underdeveloped, causes almost as much emotional stress as the thwarting of overdeveloped instincts.

A case clearly illustrating this came to our notice in a Western city some years ago.

An ambitious young woman had risen to a very responsible position for one of her youth — private secretary to the president of a large importing house. But she became so ill-tempered that her employer finally told her she could have a month in which to redeem herself, at the end of which time she must leave unless her disposition had improved.

She was especially chagrined at this for she had only a few months before been promoted to the position after years of keeping her eye on it as her goal.

She adapted herself easily to all the duties save one: The president insisted that the new secretary take his dictation herself.

She had done little stenography in her previous position, but was in practice and got out the letters in expert fashion. But after each dictation period she was so emotional that the merest trifles caused her to cry or scold or laugh hilariously.

When she came to us she was on the verge of a nervous breakdown, due to the suppression of one instinct, and to the demand for another which in her was but little developed.

The overdeveloped instinct was that of approbation. She demanded constant praise, and had always received much of it from previous employers. The president was not given to compliments and no matter how excellent her work, never told her it was so nor seemed to be aware that she was a remarkably competent secretary.

She was also very pretty and this was the first employer who had not, in some nice, indirect way, taken notice of this fact.

In addition to this, he dictated much more rapidly than she had been accustomed to and though she got every word and punctuated correctly, it was at the cost of intense effort, because she had very little of the instinct of manipulation upon which easy hand work depends.

Inertia and Indolence

An intellectual and charming woman of thirty-five, who had taught in Columbia for several years, decided to put her knowledge to a wider use and one which would bring her better financial returns.

She entered into a partnership with another college woman and they were very successful.

The other woman was full of common sense and practicality as well as learning. She was, moreover, a bundle of energy. She loved the work and never tired of it — retiring at one in the morning and arising at six more refreshed than the other who usually retired several hours earlier.

Though their work was but a few hours in duration it began at eight o'clock each morning. The first woman was always late.

She could not bring herself to get out of bed, and must take a warm bath in which she lay relaxed for twenty minutes before bringing herself to dress, and became very angry if warned to hasten.

She finally returned to the teaching where her working hours were in the middle of the day.

When relating the experience after studying Mental Analysis she said, " I used to become so furious with my partner when she urged me to get up early, hasten through my bath or sit up after ten o'clock that I was ill afterward. I had never been compelled to hurry or rise earlier than eight, and my half hour of relaxation in the bath was as much a part of my day's schedule as meals, and much more necessary to my peace of mind.

"I blamed myself for losing my temper, especially as she was right and our success depended upon my being prompt, but that didn't help matters. I know why now. The instinct of inertia is overdeveloped in me. I can work long and hard once I am up and out, but I demand frequent periods of complete relaxation, lots of sleep and to begin the day with that feeling of utter comfort which nothing but a warm bath gives."

The Wife's Story

A wife found that she was losing her husband because of her frequent emotional explosions. She made all manner of sacrifices for him — loved him devotedly, and permitted him to impose on her in numberless ways. But when he dropped cigar-ash on the carpet, left his newspapers strewn over things, threw his towels in a wad on the bathroom floor, or failed to hang up his clothes, she flew into a rage. She could not explain it.

That the emotion was out of all proportion to the importance of the thing itself, she well knew. What she did not know was that the home-keeping instinct which man shares with all birds, beavers and nest-building creatures was overdeveloped in her.

Her one desire in life was to keep her home nest in apple-pie order. She had married a man who had so little of this instinct that her ill temper on these occasions seemed to him nothing short of insanity. She gradually learned to use that emotional current to tidy up the house that much sooner, instead of expending it on her husband.

The Mother's Story

"I What shall I do about my boy?" a mother said. " I try so hard to please him. I cook only the food he likes; I wait upon him and adapt myself and the household to his wishes. But he seems to hate me."

The boy admitted all this and his shame at the treatment he gave his mother, but said she unknowingly did one thing which so irritated him that he was actually growing to hate her.

"She is always afraid — afraid of the future for me and for herself. She is afraid we may get ill; afraid she is getting a cold; afraid that it is going to storm; afraid that something will happen to one or both of us.

"Now I am afraid too, but I am trying to keep my fear to myself, to forget it and outgrow it. But she waves it in front of me all the time and I can't forget. I am not naturally self-confident. I suppose I get this fear-attitude from her. I am sorry she suffers from it, for I suffer too. But her insistence on holding every kind of catastrophe before my imagination enrages me more and more."

The mother, when told what ailed her son, was completely taken back. She had "only done it for his good," — to warn him and induce him to be prepared for the exigencies of life. A little lesson on how to cure worry changed her and the son and the household in a month's time.

Higher Emotions

But not all emotions are inimical ones. Those of love, patriotism and religion show how an emotion can stimulate and purify the personality.

Sympathy, forgiveness, generosity and all forms of humanitarianism are good emotions which lift us far out of our small selves, and give us the joy of being all human for hours or days at a time.

Every kind word, every courageous deed, every act of voluntary self-sacrifice, is full of emotion. Every pioneer, every trail-blazer in any line of endeavor goes on and on in the face of difficulties which seem overwhelming to other men, because he is sustained by an emotion they do not feel.

The mother gives of herself, her love, service, toil and life itself, all for the emotion of mother love. The father works long hours at uncongenial tasks, not actually for the boss but for the wife and babies at home.

Knowing Yourself Better

The first step in conquering destructive emotions and encouraging constructive ones is to study yourself.

Begin to think of yourself as you are and as you know you are, without whimpers or pretences. But don't let anything in your nature cause you to give up. Look it square in the eye and half the trouble is over.

We handicap ourselves by putting on the blinders of self-evasion. We refuse to be frank with ourselves. We subconsciously know we are full of faults but we exaggerate some and ignore others.

Some of the emotions you possess could, if capitalized, make you a real success in life. But you have not thought of emotion as having any such power. The world has not recognized it until very recently. History and biography dwell on the less significant elements of its great men and women, forgetting or leaving to the poets the emotional qualities which are at the foundation of every famous name.

Don't Be Supersensitive

The opposite extreme are those who imagine emotionalism alone is something to be proud of. Such people pride themselves on their sensitiveness, their "high strung" natures — forgetting that only as we *direct* our emotions into worth-while channels for accomplishment, for the good of ourselves and our fellows, can strong emotions become an asset.

Every organism, to live, must be sensitive to the stimuli in its environment. But if it is too sensitive it will forever be in the business of dressing its wounds and have time for little else.

Supersensitive people are like the little flowers called " sensitive plants" which curl up at the merest touch. They are always looking at their feelings with a microscope. Others are just as emotional but spend their feelings outward and upward like a sunflower that is so enthusiastic about the sun it turns its face from East to West each day to keep looking at it.

Use Your Emotions

Your character is the result of your conduct. Your conduct is the outward expression of your inner emotions. If you desire a strong and beautiful character you must learn to use your emotions toward building the things you want to come true in your life.

Though it is not an easy thing to believe, it is nevertheless true that we can apply our emotions to good ends. We can turn their current into positive channels where it will, like the torrent of Niagara, furnish power for doing many big things we cannot do by reason alone.

Whenever you have a destructive emotion don't swallow it and try to forget it. Don't hate or love a thing, desire to do or crave not to do a thing, and sit still. Get up while the mood is on and do something you have been neglecting.

One of the ablest men I have ever known told me he had mastered three languages by carrying a little grammar in his pocket and studying it while waiting for his wife in the hall, on the street corner or wherever he had an engagement to meet her.

"The first five years after we were married I, who am a naturally prompt person myself, was so incensed at her unvarying tardiness it threatened to wreck our marriage. She could never understand my ravings. Each time she felt she had been unavoidably detained. I was ill sometimes for days after one of these explosions.

"When I realized I could never change her I hit upon this idea of improving the time. This was my wife's one serious fault. We have been ideally happy for thirty years since — in which time I have not only learned these new languages but read and digested much of the world's best literature."

This is but one of thousands of possible ways in which an emotion and a period of precious time, which would otherwise be used to tear down, can be made to build up.

Choose Your Emotions

Just as surely as you can use your emotions after they are aroused you can prevent the wrong ones being aroused most of the time, by learning, as you will in the last lesson of this course, how to gain conscious control of the attitudes which bring forth your habitual emotions.

It is these habitual explosions that endanger our happiness. They can be made constructive instead of destructive by changing our predominant mental attitudes from negative to positive — an accomplishment perfectly possible to any person of average intelligence.

By Elsie Lincoln Benedict and Ralph Paine Benedict

Fear is the twin of Faith's sworn foe, Distrust.
If one breaks in your heart the other must.

Fear is the open enemy of Good.
It means the God in man misunderstood.

Who walks with Fear adown life's road will meet
His boon companions, Failure and Defeat.

But look the bully boldly in the eyes
With mien undaunted, and he turns and flies.

Lesson III
Dissolving Our Fixed Fears

In the back of his mind, each individual has a mass of fixed preferences and prejudices.

The fundamental predilections of his nature are due to his type and are held in common with all others of that type. Their origin is biological, as has been fully treated in our course, "The Five Human Types."

But in addition to these, and alongside of them, there are myriads of little attitudes peculiar and personal to each and every individual and which come from his training, his education, his environment and his experience.

Beans and Apples

To realize the difference between the biological foundations of your nature — the things that make you in the by-and-large — and the hundreds of inclinations and indispositions which are privately and personally "your own make," you might visualize a half bushel basket full of apples. These are your type traits. They make up your fundamentals.

But after the basket is as full of apples as it will hold you can pour into the chinks a very large amount of navy beans. These are akin to the personal peculiarities which "fill in" the main outline called You.

In every individual over five years of age there are literally thousands of these miniature but mighty eccentricities which help or hinder us. They vary as widely and exist as universally as the human beings who possess them — which helps to account for the fact that no two people in the world are exactly alike.

Where They Come From

The average man, though he possesses — and is only too often possessed by — these automatic attitudes, seldom realizes their existence in his subconscious, much less conceives of their causes. He often imagines he makes his decisions volitionally, when his friends have long since learned that under certain circumstances he is sure to react a certain way.

He always gives reasons and he is perfectly sincere in imagining these reasons are the real foundation of his decisions.

But a mass of complicated machinery run by very definite psychological and physiological forces, of which he is entirely unconscious, really works out the reaction he gives to almost every situation.

He knows little or nothing about psychology and so neither sees his mental wheels go round nor even dreams of the vast plant in which they operate.

Origin of Fixed Feelings

As before explained, we get the main fundamentals of our natures — the outlines — from our biological type. But the dents, fancies, faiths and fears are impressed on us by environment.

There are three kinds of fixed feelings — fixed fears, fixed faiths and fixed fancies.

Every fixed fear comes from an experience which produced so painful an emotion that the memory sank deep into the subconscious mind.

The reason we are so often unconscious of the origin of these fixed feelings is, as stated earlier, that the conscious mind deals in thoughts but the subconscious in feelings; and because they usually arise from experiences which occurred in childhood before the conscious mind was developed. But the subconscious, being thoroughly alive even in babyhood, remembers the emotion while the conscious one *forgets the cause.*

The more intense any feeling (emotion) the more does the conscious mind tend to forget it. This is true for two very interesting reasons.

The first is, that since we cannot think deeply and feel deeply at the same moment, any intense emotion (feeling) temporarily dethrones the conscious thinking mind and thus prevents its having a very clear conscious memory of what happens.

(You will note how little you can recall of the things you did or said during excitement or any intense emotion).

The subconscious (which never forgets anything and especially never forgets an emotion), is deeply concerned with every emotional experience. Every intensely emotional experience makes an impression so deep that its permanent mark is left on the subconscious. Secondly, to be reminded of any deep emotion so interferes with the work of the conscious mind that it is automatically on the defensive.

Psychology of Fixed Fears

When an emotion is extremely painful a scar is left which is easily irritated ever after by anything which reminds the subconscious of the original pain.

We so often have revulsions of feeling against people and things without in the least knowing why. Whenever this happens it is because the person or thing which you automatically dislike — while doubtless innocent in itself — *bears a resemblance to the symbol* by which the old painful experience was recorded in the subconscious.

The subconscious, as you will recall, does not deal in thoughts nor details but reduces everything to simple symbols which ever afterward stand for the original.

Why You Dislike People

When, for instance, you take an instantaneous dislike to an individual, even before you have spoken to him, it is because he brings up the symbol of some past painful emotional experience.

The way he combs his hair, or the tilt of his ear, may bring up the old ugly picture subconsciously. You may never have noticed that the person you disliked combed his hair that way and you may not be consciously aware now that the present man does, but the subconscious noted it in the first man and is reminded of it by the second.

Foolish as all this seems to practical everyday souls, it is invariably the real reason. The conscious mind is not so impressionable but remember, the conscious mind *reasons* whereas the subconscious *feels* — and that, blindly.

This illustration holds good only concerning people whom you dislike *instantaneously*.

Laws of Our Personal Dislikes

The following little rules will clarify the reasons for your likes and dislikes of people.

When you dislike a stranger *instantaneously* and *before he has spoken*, it is because something about him reminds you of the symbol of a painful experience.

When you dislike a stranger *after the first five minutes of conversation* with him it is because of *his personality*.

When you dislike him after *long acquaintance* it is because *his type conflicts with yours*.

Psychology of Fixed Faiths

Faith is the opposite of fear. It operates in exactly the opposite manner on the mind, body and spirit of man. Faith is a stimulant, fear a deadly narcotic. Faith is food, fear is poison. Faith develops, fear destroys.

Recalling again that the subconscious does not *think* but *feels* and that faith is a feeling, you will see why faith has been necessary to the uplift of mankind.

Thoughts are cold things compared with feelings and "the faith that moves mountains" is always a matter of heart more than head.

Law of Fixed Faiths

Every fixed faith comes from one or many experiences which produced emotions so pleasing and uplifting that the memory of them sank deep into the subconscious mind.

This accounts for the fact that cold logic never swerved any man from any religious faith which had fully satisfied him in times of need.

Conversely, no man was ever completely won to any religious faith till his emotions had been appealed to, no matter how logical the evangelist.

No public speaker ever became famous on his reasoning. His "heart as well as his head" had to talk. We are creatures of feeling

By Elsie Lincoln Benedict and Ralph Paine Benedict

much more than thinking; but our success in life depends upon directing our feelings by thinking.

When You Like People

All of us are swayed in favor of certain people purely upon our feelings. We see men and women whom we instantaneously like or even love, without being able to tell why.

They may have none of the qualities we have always supposed necessary to the winning of our love, just as the other person we disliked may have had them all — but we love them — that's all.

This illuminating new science of Mental Analysis shows us it is no accident that we instantaneously like or love another person. Whenever this happens it is because that person reminds the subconscious of a symbol which stands for some *highly pleasurable emotion* or group of pleasurable emotions in our past experience.

Woman in the Fur Hat

A man of our acquaintance who owned a grocery store told us that for thirty years he had made it a point to wait on every woman who came into his store wearing a fur hat.

No matter what he was doing he let a clerk take his customer and gave his attention to the fur-hatted woman.

He had just one other fixed feeling and it was of an opposite nature. Whenever a man came in wearing an oil coat he waited on him only if there was no one else to do it and hustled him out as quickly as possible.

He had no idea of the origin of these fixed attitudes till the above explanation was made. Next day he recalled vividly two experiences which he had not remembered for many years and which had given rise to the fixations.

As a boy he had lived in Canada where the winters were long and severe. His mother, whom he adored and who died when he was seven, always wore a fur hat in the winter months (a fact which he did not consciously remember, but which was corroborated by her photographs and by his uncle, the mother's brother, with whom he lived).

65

Into his childish and sensitive subconscious had gone the memory of those happy emotions which his mother had given him, and all of which were symbolized by a woman in a fur hat.

The Man in the Oil Coat

The explanation of his repugnance to men in oil coats was equally easy to analyze, once he was given a clue to his subconscious.

His father, though a predominantly kind man, was a very austere one and as a boy he had been very much afraid of him. His father often threatened to punish him but he could remember only one time when he did so and that was one time when he did not deserve it.

The father accused him of taking an ax to the woods and losing it when, as a matter of fact, he had not touched the ax and had seen his father take it away himself that morning. The father denied this and gave the boy a severe whipping.

When he did so he had just come in from looking everywhere for the ax and still wore his heavy oil coat. "I never smell an oil coat without experiencing the same sufferings I had during the few moments my father was lashing me."

In this case the oil coat had become, in an emotional moment, the symbol of injustice, unhappiness, punishment and disgrace.

Popular Fixed Fears

Superstition against "Friday the Thirteenth,' refusal to walk under ladders, hatred of having one's path crossed by a black cat, fear of raising an umbrella indoors, the superstition against going back home to get something without sitting down to count ten, and the certainty that breaking a mirror means "seven years of bad luck" are a few of the most widespread and popular fixed fears.

Almost every man and woman has one or more of these ancient superstitions so deeply planted in his mind that he would just a little rather avoid them.

The only thing that can be said about them is that they belong to the Dark Ages.

Psychology of Fixing Fancies

But all our fixed feelings are not of an intensely happy or unhappy nature. Many of them are tinged only with sufficient pleasurable feeling to make us know we have a definite preference, not necessarily a faith.

On the other hand, we may have just enough prejudice against a person or thing to experience a vague unrest or the merest opposition, without its being sufficiently poignant to be called a fear. But always an instantaneous opposition, however slight, is the result of some previous painful emotion.

Fear of Knives

A woman was obsessed by a fear of everything with a cutting edge. She could not work at her kitchen table so long as the butcher knife was in sight. Whenever she had to use it for cutting bread or cake she put it away as soon as possible.

If her scissors fell into her lap while sewing she could not take another stitch until she had removed them.

Whenever her husband or sons left their razors on the wash-basin in the bathroom she was ill half the morning.

If she saw a penknife on the desk when writing a letter she could not go on until she had put it in a drawer, and then was usually too upset to finish.

This condition had persisted since before she could remember, and was getting worse. The husband, after ten years of trying to cure her of it by telling her to "forget it," had finally accepted her strange fear and was careful to put all such things out of sight.

But their four sons were now grown and all living at home. They could never remember Mother's freakish terror and left their razors and knives about where she was constantly coming in contact with them.

She was told by the Mental Analyst that this obsession was nothing more nor less than a fear fixed in her subconscious by some past painful experience in which a sharp- edged instrument had figured and which had ever since been a symbol of that painful emotion

She was asked to let the matter lie fallow in her mind for a few days; to make no special effort to remember but to leave her memory free to recall anything connected with such an experience which might account for it. We saw her every day for a week but she could remember no incident of the kind.

Her disturbance at not having been able to recall anything proved that she had been straining her conscious mind — the very opposite of the proper method.

We told her to loosen her mental grip and let her mind drift for a few days or even weeks — until the memory came of its own accord.

Explanation of the Fear

In a few days she returned. She had dug up from her subconscious the recollection which fully explained the obsession.

In her childhood her parents had been very poor. When she was three they lived in a tumbledown house where the windows had no catches and, to be kept open, had to be held up with sticks or other things.

One Summer day, for lack of anything else, the mother had propped up a window in the kitchen with a long butcher knife. A few minutes later she had seen her baby sister, whom she dearly loved, push the knife over, and in doing so permitted the window to fall upon the knife whose blade laid the baby's palm wide open.

Fear of Sirens and Sawdust

But does not always choose such obvious elements as symbols and frequently chooses less significant ones instead of the outstanding things we might expect.

This is aptly illustrated in the case of a woman who had two terrors, neither of which seemed to bear any relation to the other or to anything she could recall.

She was forced to the conclusion that she needed an analysis when she discovered she could not enjoy her new home — a beautiful frame house in a Middle-Western town — because of her long-standing dislike of the smell of new lumber.

They had moved into the house before it was finished and the odor of the pine boards became unbearable. Her husband suggested that she take a trip, that she was nervous and overwrought, but it was impossible for her to leave just as the new furniture and hangings were to be installed.

One other thing had greatly disturbed her — the fire siren.

This was one of those small towns where a steam whistle is used for a fire-alarm. The new home was within a block of the factory whose siren was used for this purpose. Its screech was deafening, and left her nervous for hours afterward.

When told that these fears were from something which had happened in her past and doubtless in her childhood, she could recall nothing at the moment. But next day she related this story which was afterward corroborated by her sister

Its details came out as vividly as though it had happened the day before, which was not as surprising as it sounds. Though her subconscious had kept the memory below the threshold of her conscious mind, this secret hiding of it had caused it to be etched in with even greater vividness than it would otherwise have been.

This woman had grown up in a lumber camp. When about four years of age she had witnessed an accident at the sawmill. One of the men, in handling the logs, had slipped, lost his balance and had his foot carried with the log into the saw.

She had seen him fall, and almost died of fright as the great jagged saw-teeth sliced his foot from the ankle. She saw it fall off into the sawdust. Ever after the smell of lumber and the sight of sawdust were subconscious symbols of that experience.

Her aversion to sirens and other screeching noises was as obvious as the other elements, when we recall that this peculiarly shrill scream of the saw accompanies every cut into a log.

She was so much more taken up with the awful sight that she was not conscious of having heard the screech of the saw at the moment of the accident, but the subconscious recorded it as part of the symbol.

When this memory was allowed to air itself fully the obsession began to fade and in a few months had entirely disappeared.

A Man's Story

A Minneapolis man caused much comment among his friends a few years ago. He was handsome, had more than average means, was much sought after by women, equally popular among men, and a success in business. He was fastidious in his dress and person to the point of eccentricity. Any one of a dozen wealthy and beautiful society girls would gladly have accepted him in marriage. But he seemed to have no serious affairs of the heart, though he paid homage to many women.

At thirty-six he met a young professional woman, a law student, who wore her hair cropped short like a man's and who dressed in extremely mannish fashion. They were married two weeks afterward.

The man was as much mystified as his friends at his strange attraction, and the only explanation he could give was this:

"I have always had a fixed fear of long human hair. Since I was a small boy I have never seen a long, loose hair lying on anything without its disgusting me. Occasionally when a stray one came home inside my shirt with my laundry it made me actually ill.

"I have never known why I had this queer aversion and all my friends laugh at me for it. I laugh at myself, but that doesn't help matters.

"In my youth when women wore their hair fluffy and flying about the face, I was terrified whenever I was with a young woman, for fear one of those long, silky hairs would attach itself to me. I liked several girls tremendously, but the fear of ever touching that long hair prevented my ever falling really in love.

"The young law student was a girl of brains, personality and native good looks. We had the same tastes and ideas. She was no more interesting in many ways than some of the young society girls I had met, but I loved her short hair.

"I have been ideally happy in my marriage. My wife, now that she has given up law, and since she knows her short hair is a handicap to me as well as herself, wants to let it grow. She has discarded the mannish clothes and naturally the short hair is incongruous. But I cannot bear the notion, nor explain why."

He was told the law of fixed fears and in about a week recalled an incident of his childhood which he had not consciously remembered for many years but which fully explained the complex and in the end cleared it up to the place where he was willing for his wife to have long hair.

When he was a small boy — somewhere between five and seven — he and his younger sister were playing one day in the woodshed where the laundress was doing the family washing.

This was in the days of the washboard and old fashioned tubs to which were attached the big rollers for wringing clothes.

The baby sister, who had very long hair, dropped her ball into the tub, ran and leaned over to rescue it, just as the laundress was ready to put a handful of clothes through the wringer.

The baby's curls were carried into it and she was lifted off the floor by her hair and suspended there for what was a terrified moment before the boy could make the laundress thoroughly understand what was wrong.

The Strain of Music

But every individual has, in addition to these painful ones, hundreds of pleasurable fixations which give him enjoyment.

You have preferences of many kinds which are as intense as they are inexplicable.

One woman of our acquaintance loves a certain strain of Dvorak's "Humoresque" so much that she is filled with ecstasy every time she hears it and keeps it on her Victrola to play whenever she is depressed or unhappy about anything.

The first time she heard it was one night in the dining room of the Biltmore just after the theater. The young man whom she loved and is now married to, had taken her there to supper. He proposed to her as the orchestra was playing this selection.

The Linen Handkerchief

A noted business man of Kansas City who prides himself on his hardheadedness keeps twenty clean handkerchiefs in the right hand drawer of his private desk because he finds he can talk big deals over with much more confidence if, at the moment of opening the discussion, he can also open up a crisp, creased, perfectly fresh handkerchief.

But handkerchiefs are not mere handkerchiefs to him. Indeed, they are a very great deal more.

He declares they have a personality all their own. The only kind he will use are those of the severest plainness but of pure linen. Whenever he is presented with one bearing an initial, a fancy border or a touch of color — different in any way from the kind he prefers — he not only does not use it but is upset till he has disposed of it.

The fact that this man cannot remember what caused all this does not alter the law. Somewhere in his past he had a very pleasant emotional experience in which there figured a crisp, clean linen handkerchief.

The Cuckoo Clock

An interesting illustration of how something which has been a symbol of a painful emotion can later become symbolic of a pleasant one is seen in the following.

In Denver in 1909, lived a splendid and sensible young woman who had one little fixation. Owing to an unpleasant experience with a cuckoo clock years before, she could not bear the ticking of watches or clocks.

She held an important position in which she needed a watch but instead of wearing it, hung it up on the wall as far away from her desk as she could see its hands.

She would not own a clock and at night put the watch under her sofa pillows at the far end of her room. This condition had persisted for fifteen years. Then the young man who is now her husband and whom she was deeply in love with at the time, went to California and wanted someone to keep his valuable cuckoo clock for him while away. The young woman not only put it up in her room, but loved its ticking, cuckooing and everything else.

When teased about the sudden change she declared its noises were entirely different from those of all other clocks, and that it seemed to say, "Julius, Julius, Julius'" (the young man's name), with every swing of the pendulum. It had been so long associated with

72

him that to her, in his absence, it became a living symbol of her lover. The memory of the old unpleasant emotion was erased and has not returned.

In the lesson "Love, Courtship and Marriage" the effect of symbols on our loves will be taken up more fully. The aim here is to give a few illustrations of the power of all kinds of symbols in our lives.

The Heliotrope Perfume

A Chicago banker of fifty, conservative, conventional to a degree, and so austere as to be almost formidable, has one fixed preference.

He loves heliotrope and, though consciously despising the use of perfume, especially by men, must have a drop or two applied to his tie every morning before he can go to the bank. If he forgets it he makes his chauffeur turn around and take him home to get it.

He has had a standing order with his florist for twenty years, and every day before noon a small sprig of heliotrope is delivered, put into an exquisite little vase and placed by his secretary at a certain spot on his desk.

One day last year this secretary met with a sudden accident and was sent home from the office before he had arranged the flowers. In the excitement the little package containing the flowers was put into the taxi with him and carried away.

The banker told us himself that though some of the biggest bank heads in Chicago were in his office at that moment for a discussion concerning a loan of two million, and every moment important to them all, he could not begin the conference until a new bouquet had been obtained and placed in its vase at exactly the proper angle in front of him.

"I am fully aware and always have been of the origin of this fixation, though I have never told anyone before. As you know, I am unmarried but, as you probably do not know, I shall always remain unmarried. I have loved but one woman.

"She loved me in return. I was not a young, impressionable boy but a man past thirty when I met and cared for her.

73

"She always used heliotrope perfume and the first time I ever saw her a sprig of these little flowers was pinned to her muff. She died.

"To me she lives whenever I breathe this exquisite odor. I would not wish to live myself if I could not have it near me. I have felt this way for twenty years."

Strange Fixations

There are many people who have freakish fixations which they cannot explain and which, unless they cause trouble, need not be traced to their source. They should, how-ever, be cleared up if they become obsessions.

One such case is that of a man who never steps on a crack in the sidewalk. He cannot carry on a coherent conversation when walking with you down the street because he is so concentrated on avoiding the cracks in the cement or boards.

A Post Fixation

A Philadelphia minister says that for twenty years he has not been able to pass a gate post, a hitching post or a fence post without wanting to kick it.

"Last Winter," he said, " the Bishop was in the city for a few days and we were entertaining him at our home. I hoped I might be able to avoid going near any posts while with him and engaged a car to take us wherever he wanted to go.

"But the last day of his stay was sunny. He wanted to go for a walk, and insisted on its being down an avenue of fine old residences in front of many of which still stand the hitching posts of the pre-automobile era.

"For the first block I managed to keep from kicking these things, but half way down the second one I had to step over and touch one with my foot.

"The impulse was overwhelming. I said something about knocking some snow off my shoe and managed, by turning into another street at the next corner, to get along without doing it again. But I had to do it that once, regardless."

By Elsie Lincoln Benedict and Ralph Paine Benedict

Pin Fixations

Many people cannot walk past a pin on the floor; others cannot resist the temptation to look at every scrap of paper they see on the sidewalk. Others cannot walk or drive without continuously counting the change in their pockets. Others must count the steps on every staircase they climb and know the number in every stairway of every home they frequent.

We know a man in Washington, D. C, who can tell you the number of steps leading into every government building in that city, and also the exact number in every stairway in the U. S. Senate.

A woman in Seattle said she never listened to a lecturer without counting the number of steps he took, from the moment he appeared till he left the platform.

A man in Indianapolis said he had counted every gesture made by a certain lecturer during a six weeks' engagement and had filled a notebook describing them.

This was not due to any special interest in the lecturer. He had done the same for every speaker he had listened to for many years.

Origin of Strange Fixations

Every person with a freakish fixation such as these just described has acquired these strange avenues of expression because he was denied more normal outlets. Many of the normal instincts have had to be repressed.

The minister who kicks posts lived for several years in China as a missionary and as it was difficult for him to learn the language, was denied almost all companionship. He acquired this habit there.

The man who counts the steps in Washington was disappointed in love years ago and in the preoccupation which submerged him at the time unconsciously acquired this habit.

Every person who, for any reason, is driven in upon himself breaks out again through channels which are slightly or extremely abnormal — depending on the type of individual and the severity of his suffering.

"Keeping the Faiths"

If your fixed feelings are fixed *faiths* — that is, if they reassure you, uplift you, sustain you, and help you to live a better, happier life, do not let anything or anybody take them away from you.

If they are fixed fancies of a pleasing sort, such as the preference for heliotrope which the banker has, by all means keep them.

Life is all too drab and difficult not to brighten it by these innocent and purifying means whenever possible.

One Woman's Fixed Faith

A woman of our acquaintance who took her own part with great gusto in everything else permitted people to impose on her in just one way.

She allowed them to push past her into street cars, subways and all manner of other places. She gave up her place with no resistance whatever, seeming almost pleased to do so.

When asked for the cause of the strange inconsistency she said:

"Four times my life has been saved because I lost a place in line. Twice it caused me to miss a train — once because the man in front of me at the Pullman window dropped his change and tickets and kept me waiting while he gathered them up; and once because the baggage man did not get my trunk checked in time.

"Both these trains were wrecked.

"At another time I was refused admittance to a packed elevator. I was in a hurry and insisted on getting in. The fact that a large woman who was standing behind me was permitted to enter it did not lessen my anger.

"The operator lost control of his car which was overcrowded, and it dropped eight stories, killing instantly every person in it.

"The day of the historic Iroquois Theater fire in Chicago I was standing in line for a ticket when I discovered I had lost my purse and stepped out of line to find it. By doing so I lost the chance to see the play.

"If I had not lost my place I would doubtless have been among the hundreds burned alive in that awful disaster.

76

By Elsie Lincoln Benedict and Ralph Paine Benedict

"Now whenever I lose a place in line I believe it is for some good purpose."

Bonaparte's firm faith that "the bullet had not been cast nor the shell tempered that could kill Napoleon" not only filled the minds of his enemies with fear of even attempting it, but carried him to many victories.

Freeing Yourself of Fixed Fears

But if you have fixed fears of any nature you must master them or run the risk of their mastering you.

Nothing in nature remains stationary. The moment you are not getting stronger you are getting weaker. The man who stops climbing has begun to slide back.

To live a healthful, happy, honorable life you must be master of your moods. To be master of your moods, the first thing to do is: face the fact and begin to be honest and sensible.

Mental Analysis, this most searching and profound of all human sciences, has proved that most of our worst mental and physical ailments, disappointments and failures come from our refusal to be frank and straightforward with ourselves.

Whether the thing you are afraid of is big or little, real or imaginary, you can be free from it if you try.

You are one of God's creatures and God never meant any creature to be sad, dejected or frightened. We make ourselves so by violating His divine laws.

Renovating the Subconscious

If your obsessions are those of regret for past sins of commission or omission, try to think of this subconscious of yours as a pool that you are going to drain by being perfectly honest with yourself.

And you *can* be because nothing you have ever done, thought, said or been guilty of was so very bad.

The force that rules the universe is big, beautiful, and above all, benign. A benign force, whether personal or impersonal, forgives or ignores our faults. Put yourself in harmony with the divine by forgiving yourself right now for anything that has been causing you regret or remorse.

No matter what you have done or failed to do, just remember this: you did the best your nature was capable of at that time, under those conditions, and with those particular temptations.

The worse it was the more is it necessary that you do that much better in the future.

You cannot do anything big or fine with fear gripping and crippling you.

Whatever negative thing is in your mind and however long it may have been there, it can be eliminated by doing two things:

First, be honest with yourself. Admit to yourself that you have been a weak, silly fool or anything else that you have been. But don't let it discourage you.

Confession is good for the soul. It clears the air. It blows the cobwebs out of your mind. It is a mental vacuum cleaner.

Second, realize that whatever you desire to come true in your life can be brought to pass if you really *want it.*

It can be brought to pass by the same power that has brought most of the things you have in your life — your own sub-conscious mind.

It will not do so in a day. The subconscious does not respond to a thought until many times repeated. The only thing it reacts to instantly is *feeling.* But through a law which is fully explained in the last lesson of this course, any desired impulse can be planted in the subconscious.

Once there, it will operate with the same unresting force as these other urges of ours which have been shot into it by emotion.

You can plant in your subconscious soil the seeds of anything you truly desire. It will bring forth its harvest according to its nature.

You must stop filling this great battery with negative energy.

By right thinking you can make all its energy positive, and that positive force will bring to pass whatever you deeply desire.

By Elsie Lincoln Benedict and Ralph Paine Benedict

Mind is the master power
That molds and makes,
And man IS mind,
And evermore he takes
The tool of thought
And shaping what he wills.
Brings forth a thousand joys
Or a thousand ills.
He thinks in secret
And it comes to pass,
Environment is just
His looking-glass.

Lesson IV
Mental Miracles

Man is a unit. Each human being is an organized community of living cells, of which there are over twenty-six trillions in the commonwealth of the
brain and body.

This intricate and intimate relationship between all the cells of the human organism is effected through two channels — the nervous system and the circulatory system.

The living cables of the nervous system run from the brain through the spinal cord and solar plexus; and branch and rebranch until practically every cell in the body has its own tiny nerve.

By means of this sensitive system any part of the brain or body instantly influences — for health or disease, happiness or distress — every other part of the organism.

Nerve Messengers

To illustrate to yourself how quickly and keenly the outside world, without tangible contact, affects the body through this delicate nervous system, recall what happened to you when you have smelled something extremely disagreeable.

The impression was carried to the brain which instantly sent over its nerve-wires a mental telegram to your stomach. If it was very unpleasant you became nauseated.

If the revulsion was severe there resulted those violent convulsions of the stomach which cause vomiting.

Yet you had neither touched nor tasted the unpleasant thing — merely heard of it through your nerves.

Chemical Messengers

The next day you are passing a bakery. You smell the delicious odor of bread. The brain dispatches a pleasing telegram to your stomach telling it to secrete the gastric juices preparatory to digesting some of that bread.

You instantly become hungry. If you cannot stop and get a loaf to take home or eat it then and there — if you keep on going and ignore it — an interesting thing happens.

The juices which ran into your stomach on that hurry call have no food to work on. Since their energy (like that of everything else) must expend itself, they agitate your empty stomach — an abnormal process, which in turn makes you slightly physically and then mentally upset.

When that point is reached the circle is completed; you are back to the mind from whence the message first came.

Your body and mind always operate in this circle. Whatever affects one affects the other.

A mental disturbance not only harms the body but, because the body also affects the mind, comes back like a boomerang when it completes the circle.

A physical disturbance not only upsets the mental processes, but returns, via their influence, back to the body in that same vicious circle.

Human Hungers

This little hunger for the bread is only the most elemental illustration. Every normal human being has hundreds and thousands of hungers .

The particular kind most frequent and intense with each individual comes, as a bread-hunger would ultimately have come, from your own inner nature. This inner nature will show in his externals and determine his type.

But life is forever tempting, reminding, awakening these sleeping tendencies, just as the accidental passing by the bakery awakened your hunger for bread.

Type Hungers

Now if you had been excessively hungry — that is, had a deep *inner urge* for food — before you came to the bakery it would have been much more difficult for you to keep going.

By Elsie Lincoln Benedict and Ralph Paine Benedict

And so it is with our type-hungers. They come from our inner biological systems, and are quick to flare up when anything occurs in our environment which appeals to them.

But whether the hunger comes from the over-development of an inner system or is aroused by outer stimuli, any hunger which is repressed and ignored expends its pent- up energy, as did the gastric juices, on something else. Thus we have discovered the:

Law of Repression

Every intense impulse or ambition which is refused expression through normal, natural outlets, finds less normal and sometimes abnormal outlets for itself.

Today science shows that most of our unhappiness and failure and practically all our ill health, half-health and disease are but the distorted expressions of deep desires long repressed.

The Dammed-Up Stream

Your mental and physical energy is like a river. It must flow onward and outward to stay pure and natural.

A pool becomes stagnant only when denied an outlet. The most foul water purifies itself in a few miles of rapid flowing.

Society in general, and conditions or relations in which we place ourselves restrain us and choke back this natural expression as a dam holds back a river.

Such a dam holds the water back temporarily, and nothing happens.

But if the pressure becomes greater and greater, after a while one of two things *will* happen: the dam will break or the stream will burst over in another direction.

Disease and wrongdoings are often the breaking out of the subconscious stream. Reversions are the result of the breaking of the dam itself.

Causes of Crime

Criminologists declare that crime is the result of the repression of the true personality and that criminals differ from the average

83

man and woman chiefly in that a much larger proportion of the personality is thwarted.

It is well known that delinquents are invariably defective physically and often physically deformed.

Every man who has been long a criminal has one or more serious physical diseases — a fact known to all heads of jails, reform schools, penitentiaries, and to all penal and social investigators.

These and hundreds of corroborative facts prove how closely the body, mind and spirit of man are intertwined, and how everything which affects one affects the other.

What To Do

It is not necessary to dwell on these impulses in our minds nor to act them out in our lives.

Civilization has cost too much on the part of brave souls and is too great a boon to mankind for any individual to revert to the primitive where all this is lost on him.

He owes it to himself, first of all, and second to the world, to straighten his spine and live the life of a man.

We have been told this before. But we have not been told *how* to make a working compromise between these inner impulses which, for any reason, could not be expressed naturally, and the ideals we so much desired to live up to.

No one was to blame for this state of affairs. No one knew, until very recently, that choking an intense impulse *did not kill it.*

No one suspected, for instance, the real reason for the chronic ailments, soured dispositions and "queer streaks' ' of old maids of both sexes; nor why people who live alone, people who are unloved or unsuccessful, develop certain kinds of maladies, mental and physical.

About "Forgetting"

Today we know that the admonition to "forget it " merely crowds the unspent energy down into the lower reaches of the organism, from whence it emerges sooner or later in some less natural form.

The big lesson taught by Mental Analysis is that whenever you have any intense impulse which cannot or should not be expressed, you are to look it straight in the face, realize that it is no different from the impulses of millions who have gone before you; that it is not perverted, disgraceful nor anything to be ashamed of *as an impulse.*

No Self-Hate

The thing to be ashamed of would be the secret loathing of yourself for having it or permitting it to act itself out in harmful, dishonorable or destructive deeds.

After you have looked at it; after you have recognized it for the out of date or out of place impulse it is, say to this thing: "Yes, you were all right in your day, a million years ago before we learned that human progress depended on the development of the higher instincts. You are the natural descendant of the primitive in me, and as such are not to blame for being here.

"But if you think I am going to live down to your level just because you *are* here, you are very much mistaken!

"Now, you have a lot of energy. Stop whining in the dark there. Come out into the light and I'll put that energy to work. I am a twentieth century human being with a brain and I am going to live the life of one, not that of a man of dead ages.

"I have nothing against you. All you need is to expend that energy of yours. I'll find something right out here in the daylight for you to do. Get at it!"

Tender-Minded vs. Tough-Minded

As a result of our wrong systems of training the most sensitive and high-minded are often obsessed with a sense of shame and disgrace which cripples all their efforts, while the "tough-minded,"' as James called them, express more of their inner urges, accomplish more, keep their health and get the good things out of life.

They do not do this necessarily by expressing destructive urges in their original form, but often by an automatic sublimation natural to their biological type.

Other and finer types — taught by parents, teachers, preachers and society that certain things are vile — believe it and grow to despise themselves.

Psychology of Shame

No human being can stay well or do good work who secretly loathes himself.

It is small wonder that some of our orthodox churches are empty. Renunciation and repression are stunting, saddening, sickening doctrines. They weaken, disintegrate and destroy

The sense of " original sin," of an inner filth that can never be quite eliminated, is fatal to health and happiness. Of its own force, it is ultimately fatal to any sect that teaches it.

God never intended any living thing to be cowed or shamed. Everything in nature grows *up*, not down. It grows with its head toward the heavens.

When human beings listen less to men and more to the sermons in every sun-seeking flower, they will begin to be good, happy, healthy and successful.

Conscious vs. Subconscious

The average individual tries not to think or feel certain things. He crowds them out of his mind and thinks they are gone.

Today we know that whatever is pushed out of consciousness recedes into subconsciousness.

If these throttled thoughts concern deep desires they come back again and again. If rejected over and over they finally return behind the " false face" of some unaccountable attitude which we do not recognize as connected with anything we have previously felt. We now know these are merely old urges in disguise.

Most of our physical ills, emotional explosions, outbursts of temper and faults are these repressed impulses on masquerade.

Satan At Our Shoulders

As children we were taught that the way to dispose of Satan was to say, " Get thee behind me." We were told that when we did this Satan vanished.

Today the science of Mental Analysis shows what we have always suspected — that Satan stayed right there and has been talking over our shoulders ever since!

It shows us that we have got to do something besides put Satan behind our backs unless we wish to be pushed into the very things we fear.

Fortunately, it shows us that the things we must do to turn his power into constructive channels is much easier than the things we have been doing in our blind and ignorant efforts to get rid of him.

Where Faults Come From

Every human fault, like every disease, is the result of dammed-up energy.

Everything in the world moves, and does so because it is full of energy. Nothing is ever still, even for an instant, no matter how much it may appear so.

Everything — from the particles in the wooden chair on which you sit to the constellations in the sky — are moving, moving, moving.

Motion is the law of the universe. Motion creates energy and energy must expend itself.

If you do not permit it to expend itself in natural, normal ways it expends itself in abnormal, unnatural ways — depending always on the type of individual and the weakest point in his physical or mental makeup.

When you see no evil effects for a time you imagine you have obliterated this impulse.

But you have only bottled it, and the longer you keep the cork in the more it ferments. Some day it will explode.

Expression and Repression

Any work, situation or condition which compels you to keep on doing a thing you do not like to do causes the gradual building up within you of a mass of aversions and repulsions which eventually break forth.

They may not break out in open rebellion against *the thing itself*. In fact we have discovered that the greater the dislike of a

87

thing on the part of certain types of people the less likely are they to voice their resentment or to show open resistance to that specific thing.

These are the people to whom comes the greatest harm. Whenever you express open opposition to a thing you "let off steam" and relieve the pressure just that much.

The types that " speak out" have far fewer subconscious complexes than the silent, timid ones, though they often have the very ones they and their friends would least expect to find in them.

The Hidden Fires

A young boy was left alone while his mother went to the corner grocery. A box of papers he was playing with caught fire from the open grate. He was too young to know how to put out the fire and afraid to run away from it. So he ran to the back stairs, threw the blazing box into the basement and slammed the door.

He had a few moments of apparent safety.

But the house burned down.

Effect of the Wish

It used to be supposed that some men had an aim and others had not; that some knew what they wanted and others had no preferences; that some men were blessed with ambitions and others didn't care.

Today we know that every individual has many subconscious wishes and *one overwhelming subconscious longing* toward whose attainment every act of his life is consciously or unconsciously directed.

Everything which tends toward the fulfillment of this subconscious wish reacts constructively, happily, healthily back upon his body, mind, work, and life in its entirety.

Everything which hinders it reacts destructively upon every element of his personality — physical, mental, moral and spiritual — and takes its toll in some form of depression, disintegration or disease.

Minstrels and "The Merry Widow"

"An interesting illustration of how the thwarting of a subconscious wish can cause physical troubles and how quickly the removal of the barrier can cure, came to my notice in 1910," said a physician recently.

"It also shows the lesser power of conscious wishes as compared to the great force of subconscious ones.

"I was sent for at 4:30 one afternoon to come to an office in the State Capitol in Denver where a young woman was ill.

"She was suffering with intense pain and had a temperature of 103.

"It developed at five o'clock, when the rest of the office force left, that she had been very anxious to see 'The Merry Widow' which was playing at the Broadway Theater that week, and was to have gone with the rest of the girls that evening to see it.

"She was much disappointed that her illness necessitated their giving the ticket to someone else.

"While we waited for the taxi which was to take her home she told me how sorry she was not to see ' The Merry Widow' but glad she didn't have to see the minstrels which were also in town. She very much disliked minstrels, she said.

"A moment later the telephone rang and she was asked for. I told the young man at the other end of the wire that she was too ill to answer. But before I could prevent it she took up the receiver.

"Two minutes later she walked out of that room free of her headache and fever — perfectly well.

"The illness, she told me as we walked down the hall, had come from a week's worry over not having heard from the young man, whom she loved devotedly. She feared she had lost him.

" When he phoned and asked her to go that evening to the minstrel show (having already seen ' The Merry Widow' himself) she found she would love the minstrels after all; that she didn't mind missing 'The Merry Widow' and was well enough to go."

The illness in this case was real. The desire to see "The Merry Widow" and not to see the minstrels was genuine, but existed only in her conscious mind, whereas the desire to be with the young man was part of a deep subconscious wish and, as such, able to make her not only glad to see the minstrels, but to become well instantly.

Fear and Health

Fear causes more maladies, physicians say, than all other things combined. The man who is afraid is never a well man.

Strange as it may seem, it is the fears we repress more than the fears we express, which do us severe harm — another illustration of how things shoved back into subconsciousness wreak their force upon us under assumed appearances.

Fear and Epidemics

It is a historical and well-known fact that every war is followed by epidemics.

We have assumed that congestion of masses of men, poor sanitation and exposure were the inevitable causes, and certain it is that these have had much to do with it.

But hundreds of the leading physicians of the world have declared that the Spanish Influenza epidemic of 1918 was caused largely by fear in many cases and that at its height many people had every outward symptom of this disease without the slightest fever or any actually diseased condition.

They have gone a step farther and declared that patients died under the impression that they were afflicted with this malady when, as a matter of fact, they were killed by fear.

Complexes and Consciousness

It was shown in a previous lesson that fixed fears always come from very painful emotional experiences of one's past.

The insidious and far-reaching effect of a single fixed fear was explained.

Imagine then the effect upon the individual of an integrated, organized *group* of fixed fears — a "set" of them — surrounding some long drawn out or vital experience in his life.

Mental science distinguishes these groups of fixed fears by the name of complexes. They differ from others chiefly in the fact that instead of one element they have many.

Single fixed fears arise from momentary or even instantaneous experiences, such as the little girl suffered in the fraction of a second when she witnessed the saw cutting off the man's foot. Her fixed fear of screeching noises and the smell of lumber was born in that instant of intense emotion.

What can rightly be called a complex is the result of an experience of much longer duration — sometimes of years — which contained many characteristics. Several of these are symbolized in the subconscious mind with such vividness that being reminded of one brings the " total experience" forth from memory's vault.

A Husband's Complex

A Cleveland broker who had a reputation for cool-headedness and self-control developed a violent complex against women's white kid gloves, plumes, French-heeled shoes and baby-Irish lace.

Whether displayed in shops or being worn by their fair owners, whenever and wherever he saw any of these things his composure instantly left him and he grew angry, disgusted and resentful.

Though he succeeded in concealing his agitation from his friends and employees, he declared it was hours, sometimes days, before he fully recovered.

These things upset him, he said, because they brought back to him with terrific force memories of a bitter period in his life.

Many years before he had been married to a charming and unusually beautiful woman whom he idolized — the only woman moreover that ever interested him.

She flirted with other men, gave him ten years of heart-breaking disillusionment and finally eloped with a clerk of his office.

She was a woman of extremely fashionable and fastidious tastes. She specialized in French-heeled shoes, white kid gloves, and the willow plumes and baby-Irish lace which were the mode at that time.

Whenever he saw any of these things the tragedy of the whole ten years engulfed him — the " total experience' ' lived itself over in his feelings, condensed and intensified.

Not only did it remind him of the love for his wife, the scandal in the newspapers, the loneliness and shame he underwent because of her deception, it recalled the humiliation his pride had suffered at her having gone away with one of his own employees. This was a young man he had never liked and whom he had often reprimanded.

A Wife's Complex

A woman developed a complex against men smoking pipes. She had once liked the sight of a man smoking a pipe and, unlike the man just described, could not imagine why she became enraged whenever she saw a pipe in any man's mouth.

If, in addition to seeing it, she heard the slight smack of the lips as he puffed at its stem her emotion was so intense she had to leave the room or even the street car in which it was occurring.

As she was a widow and had several children to support, she found it necessary to overcome this violent aversion.

She had just been promoted to a much better paying position which she was perfectly able to fill but which she was having great difficulty with because several men at nearby desks smoked pipes during office hours.

After a time she realized that something she had faithfully pushed out of her conscious mind for years and which she had not once admitted to herself, was a fact and that this fact had given rise to the complex.

Cause of Her Complex

Her husband insisted on a large family, yet failed to support them.

He was an able man who drew a good salary at the time of their marriage. She loved him devotedly and believed him when he said he could get nothing to do later on.

He finally gave up trying to work, on the plea of not being well, and spent all his time at home, sitting by the fire, puffing away at his pipe.

He was finally killed in an automobile accident — after the wife had had twelve years of hard work trying to support their family — twelve years when her most vivid picture of him was as he looked and sounded, sitting there by the fire, smacking his lips on his pipe stem.

She had never permitted her conscious mind to harbor the suspicion that he was lazy, worthless and selfish. But the conviction of it was imbedded deep in her subconscious which had symbolized the heartaches and hardships of the whole twelve years in the scene and sound of a man smoking a pipe.

Types and Complexes

You have often wondered why two people of the same family (therefore of the same heredity) and of the same environment (living in the same house under exactly identical conditions) would react in diametrically *opposite* ways to the *same* experience.

For instance, twin sisters lose their mother through death.

One is completely overwhelmed by grief, loses weight, becomes ill and is unconsolable, while the other grows rosier and plumper every day and goes on just as before.

Why does one girl develop a complex and the other not?

Chiefly because of difference in type.

Certain types react to certain kinds of experiences destructively and others constructively, and do so habitually and automatically On the other hand, the girl who reacts with death may develop complexes from different kinds of experiences which would not affect the other girl at all.

What Happens To You

Whenever the mind is working destructively — when, for instance, you are full of fear — it throws the switch and sidetracks the body, preventing its running properly or safely.

When our emotions become tangled up with wrong ideas, destructive attitudes or opposition, they are at cross purposes with the body.

This always has its damaging results. These results may show themselves in the form of nervousness, ill temper, ill health, melancholia, neurosis, insanity, crime or suicide — always depending on the type of individual.

Or, they may merely cause him to wonder what is wrong between himself and the world; to form incomprehensible aversions to people and things in his environment; or to be vaguely restless, upset or unhappy, without knowing why.

Dreams and Diseases

Thousands of facts go to show that the dreamer weaves his own dream out of the raw materials in his own conscious experience and subconscious desires — that each dream is the dreamer's own psychic production.

This fact is of the utmost significance. It has shown the underlying causes for neuroses and other illnesses which, until the discovery of Mental Analysis, were inexplicable to physicians and supposedly incurable.

The psychologist is today curing many people of many maladies which the physician, dealing only with the body, failed to help.

"Within ten years," says a prominent surgeon, "every physician who undertakes to help a patient suffering from any functional disorder will make his first step the analysis of the patient's dreams."

Today we know that numberless operations, most organic and all functional ailments are the result of unhappiness, fear, repression or other negative mental conditions.

We know that nervous breakdowns, for instance, are due not so much to overwork as over-worry.

Reality and Regression

One of the most significant discoveries of recent times is that in every human being there is a *subconscious tendency to escape from the facts of life whenever they become too painful.*

94

By Elsie Lincoln Benedict and Ralph Paine Benedict

In scientific circles there is a new but already well-known phrase describing this: "the flight from reality "

This profound and universal fact is revolutionizing the therapeutics of the civilized world .

It is explaining all manner of mental, moral and physical maladies and curing them because it deals with the real source of the trouble,

Forms of "Flight"

The particular way taken to achieve the " flight from reality" will depend, in each case, upon the type, temperament and training of the individual and the intensity of his sufferings.

The most repressive, sensitive types suffer most because they bury their griefs and disappointments deeper than others.

Those who express their feelings suffer least from the repressive ailments, as was proven during the World War.

Soldiers and Shell-Shock[1]

Thousands of soldiers suffered from a baffling ailment. It robbed them of various phases of consciousness; it vented itself in all manner of mental derangements, with no two cases quite alike.

For the lack of a better name it was called "shell-shock," though these men had not been hurt by shells, and other men, under precisely the same conditions, had come through safely and sanely.

In many instances sight and hearing were lost, in spite of the fact that tests showed their eyes and ears to be in perfect condition.

Thousands of such cases were cured upon being removed from the scene of battle and thousands more became well in an hour after the signing of the Armistice.

What was the reason? The strange malady left as mysteriously as it came *when the danger disappeared.* In these cases fear and fear alone was responsible, say the greatest authorities now.[2]

---

[1] "Shell shock" is now known as "Post traumatic stress disorder", or PTSD.

95

Repressed Fears

It was not an open, expressed, conscious fear. Any openly expressed feeling drains off through consciousness. These shell-shocked men were of the highest human grade. They had been taught that fear is dishonorable, especially upon the field of battle.

But self-preservation is the first law of nature. Each man's subconscious mind is concerned, not with patriotism nor any other modern innovation, but with the sole business of *self-preservation* and *self-expression* for that individual.

Refusing To Run

These men refused to run or to be consciously afraid. But the subconscious was afraid and reacted with fear to that danger exactly as the hair of a cat rises when a dog comes near, and as a bird's heart beats wildly when the cat approaches.

The greatest conflict came in the consciousness of these soldiers who had the traits of conscious courage and self-preservation most highly developed. These were precisely the men who suffered most from shell-shock.

Finding a Road For Flight

Their conscious minds refused to harbor cowardice, but the subconscious, always ready to take us out of a reality that is too terrible to be borne, developed a disease that *removed the men from reality*, from danger and even from a realization of the horrors around them.

It is a matter of history now that when the steamers carrying shell-shocked men were torpedoed and the patients flung into the water, almost every man recovered his sight, hearing, reason or whatever it was he had lost — all through the subconscious powers which gave him the diseases in the first place.

---

[2] As we now know today; PTSD is not due to "fear alone" and does not "automatically" go away after the end of a war, but it is most definitely treatable.

By Elsie Lincoln Benedict and Ralph Paine Benedict

The Explanation

"The subconscious minds of these men," said a leading New York physician, " recognized in the torpedoing of the boat a new danger from which shell-shock could not save them — a danger, in fact, wherein every fiber of that organism must fight for its life. So the lost senses returned.

"The subconscious mind is the miracle mind of man! "

Dreams are the most frequent and the least harmful of these "flights from reality." Invalidism, hypochondria, drunkenness, drug-taking, all forms of neuroses and suicide itself, are but the different roads which different types and temperaments under differing conditions, take to get away from life-as-it-is.

Drugs and Dream- Worlds

In all these the conscious mind relaxes, forgets the troubles of the day, the disappointments, the hurts, the wounds — and reverts to temporary peace.

With the drugging or putting to sleep of the conscious mind the individual ceases to think. He reverts to that much more ancient and pleasurable thing — feeling.

His modern, civilized brain, which is yet so new it finds the struggle difficult, "goes off shift" and the subconscious mind — primitive, powerful, pleasing and pacifying — takes charge.

He ceases to deal with abstract thoughts or ideas.

He revels in the mental pictures supplied by the subconscious from its endless "morgue" of symbols.

Psychology of Movie Popularity

The real reason for the popularity of the modern motion picture is the fact that it appeals to an age-old instinct, an ancient psychological habit of the human race— the habit of dreaming *in pictures.*

Every person subconsciously recognizes in the motion picture the same kind of activity he has engaged in every time he dreamed a dream. Your dreams are your personal, private movie shows.

What is a "Good Movie ?"

An even deeper significance of the popularity of the moving picture lies in the fact that it furnishes in the lives of the disappointed, the depressed, the discouraged, the worried and the ailing, exactly the same relief from reality as do the dreams in our sleep — but in a lesser degree.

People unconsciously prove this by measuring every moving picture according to its ability to grip and interest them; in other words, to make them *forget reality.*

When one says he did not enjoy a certain moving picture he is unconsciously saying that, for some reason, it did not take him out of reality.

Why Tastes Differ

The fact that there are different types of people, each requiring something different to take him out of the troubles of everyday, accounts for the fact that what one calls " a great picture " is called "absolutely no good by someone else.

We unconsciously make every moving picture fill the pleasure-requirement of the dream in another vital respect — by automatically visualizing ourselves in the role of the hero or heroine. We then live the whole story vicariously, with the action revolving around ourselves.

To Test Yourself

The surest way to attain health is to renovate the mind. One way to know whether yours is building for health and happiness or for distress and disease, is to watch your own mental movies — in your daydreams and the dreams of your sleep — measuring and estimating their meaning according to the standards laid down in this lesson.

If destructive emotions pervade your sleep dreams these same emotions are disturbing your waking life and in turn your health. If you are constantly trying to escape reality you are in danger, mentally and physically. Instead of attempting to sneak out the back door, walk out through the front, into the facts of your life, and begin to change them in accordance with the last lesson in this course. This and this only will perform mental miracles for you.

We live together years and years,
And leave unsounded still
Each other's springs of hopes and fears,
Each other's depths of will.

— Lord Houghton.

By Elsie Lincoln Benedict and Ralph Paine Benedict

Lesson V
Love, Courtship and Marriage

Loving and being loved is the supremest human experience. Under its magic influence we become changed beings — happier, stronger, sweeter, better. Without it we wither, weaken and disintegrate.

Its effect on health and achievement is immeasurable. Many have attained mediocre success without visible lovers, but none ever achieved greatness without a great love. It might almost be said that none save great lovers have scaled the heights.

This does not mean that the great love of a life must necessarily be for or from one of the other sex, though these are the most powerful and productive loves possible to man

Nor does it assume that the loved one must be a flesh-and-blood creature.

The ideal whom many adore in secret and whose prototype is never found in real life, often serves greater purposes than any living lover.

"Ideal" Lovers

Very idealistic, very sensitive, very repressive types seldom find mates as beautiful, refined, sympathetic or understanding as they demand, and this accounts for the fact that these are the very types which most often remain unmated, while their opposites marry early and often.

"No one lives who is not in love, all the time, with a person, either real or ideal, " says Wilfrid Lay. "In many men and women this ideal personality is the only one loved, but often loved subconsciously, while for others there is also a consciously loved or admired real person.

"How to unite the conscious and unconscious love, so frequently at variance in the same soul, and center it upon one person of the opposite sex, becomes therefore a great problem of life today."

Love and Ego

In civilized human beings the love-urge is second to the ego-urge. In many it appears to take precedence of the direct ego-urge, though it must not be forgotten that love for an individual is always, and to a far greater extent than the lover realizes, an indirect expression of the ego.

To be loved is gratifying to the ego of every individual, regardless of whether he has ever seen or ever will see the one who loves him.

To love is to know a new power, to sense unplumbed depths in one's own soul, to realize his own strength, to express his spirit.

The Power of Love

So powerful is the effect of love that, though loving and being loved by one of the other sex is life's profoundest experience, to love and be loved by a friend, a parent, a follower, a child or even a dumb animal, is uplifting, strengthening, consoling.

This has been proven in countless cases, such as have come within the range of your own observation.

You wonder why certain men and women become so deeply attached to a dog, a bird, a cat or other pet. But to the student of Mental Analysis there is nothing strange in this phenomenon.

Love-Substitutes

Every individual craves personal love from someone, and to give out his own.

When, for any reason, he is unable to find a human being sufficiently similar to his ideal, to love and be loved by, he seeks a substitute in whatever other creature appeals to him most

Rather than being indicative of a less high evolution this often indicates a higher-than- average nature on the part of the pet-loving person.

It is well known that cruel, selfish people seldom care for animals. It is equally well known that those who are kind to animals are gentle, refined, sensitive, idealistic — in short, highly evolved men and women.

By Elsie Lincoln Benedict and Ralph Paine Benedict

These two facts are so universally known that when a motion picture introduces a character by letting you see him kick a dog or mistreating any animal you know he is the villain.

But when sweetness of nature, kindness of heart and goodness in general are to be pictured, the camera tells it all to you in a flash by showing the character petting or playing with some birds, lambs, dogs, kittens or horses.

A Cartoonist's Canary

One of the most beautiful, brilliant and famous young women in America is the cartoonist, Fay King, of whose hands we have spoken in "Realizing On Your Personality." Spirituality and gentleness of heart distinguish all her work.

In her room at the Hotel Pennsylvania, New York City, is her pet canary "Mike," whom she has had for ten years and whose imaginary sayings are familiar to the millions who see Miss King's stories and cartoons every day in the leading newspapers of the country.

Bill Hart's devotion to his beloved horse "Pinto " and Mary Pickford's to her big Danes are stronger proofs than even press agents can produce, of the natural goodness and inner refinement of these famous figures.

Freud's Sex Theory

The Freudian theory that all our activities have a sexual significance is not only disproved by the ordinary facts of our own every- day lives, but further disproved by the study of the human instincts.

Sex is a fundamental instinct and as such wields the great influence over our lives which any basic instinct wields.

But that it pervades our personal universe to the extent ascribed to it by the Viennese school seems scarcely possible, even when we allow the wide latitude and admit the great self-ignorance which the first psychoanalysts suggested

Sex Not First

In fact, measured by their effect upon our lives, a large group of instincts takes precedence of the sex instinct in the life of the average human being.

That there is a period, during adolescence, when the instinct of sex dominates our thoughts, feelings and actions, is undeniable.

But that that period of intense preoccupation with sex is of short duration is also undeniable. In the normal individual it is ordinarily not more than five years.

Even in the less-than-average lifetime there are, before it arrives and after it passes, some forty years when the instincts of assimilation, pugnacity, egoism and self-expression, — singly or combined — far overshadow the influence of the sex instinct.

Primitive Sex Symbols

With due respect to Freud, who has done so much to awaken mankind to its great subconscious forces, and whose contributions to the human sciences are immeasurable, he gives (or so it seems to some of us) undue weight to the ancient sex symbols of primitive peoples.

It is not unlikely that instead of these symbols running inward toward sex as the spokes of a wheel run into the hub, these sexual symbols were primitive attempts to picture, in the only language they knew, higher and non-sexual cravings.

Not only do we know that we have manifold and mighty impulses which are not related even remotely to sex, but we know that love itself is by no means wholly sexual — even the love between the sexes.

Love's Lure

The lure of love goes far beyond and far higher than sex lure, as we see in that greatest example of human devotion — mother-love. Every creature desires to be loved — and often to love and be loved by those with whom he cares to associate nothing sexual, even remotely.

By Elsie Lincoln Benedict and Ralph Paine Benedict

Love Cures

Alienists, physicians and psychologists are all aware of the healing power of love and the harming power of hate. We have seen many a patient cured of a disease which medical science could not touch, by the patient's falling suddenly in love. And we have seen stalwart ones succumb to all manner of maladies when thwarted in a much-desired affection.

So all-powerful and so all-pervading is the demand for love and the desire to give love that every child, so scientists say, is in love with someone by the time he is three years old. From that time to the moment of death he is in love with some real or ideal person upon whom he showers, in imagination if not in real life, the flowers of his spirit.

Parents and Children

Being instinctive, intense and impulsive, this love-urge, like every other, demands expression and, like every other, is forced to express itself in its environment.

The only environment the child knows is the home. The only people from whom it can demand love and draw love unto itself are the people in its environment.

To the average child this means his parents. They are the objects upon which he showers his own instinctive love-energy, and he tries, with all the subconscious powers he possesses, to induce them to love him in return.

None of this is reasoned nor " thought out" in any conscious sense, but is done inevitably and unerringly just as the new-born babe, consciously knowing nothing whatever, yet subconsciously knows how to satisfy hunger at its mother's breast.

The Real "First Love"

Under normal home conditions, the child finds, ready-made, the ideal situation for the growth and expression of his instinctive love- urge.

His parents, craving always more love themselves and craving always to give more love, respond not only unreservedly to the child's demand for love, but encourage its further development by doing all the things which lure love from anyone anywhere at any time since the world began.

Love begets love. It is practically impossible to resist people who truly, deeply love us and who self-sacrificingly, unselfishly continue to shower it upon us.

Thousands of marriages are consummated every year as a result of one of the pair having loved the other into loving him.

Between the child and the parent there are no barriers. Everything conduces to the encouragement, enhancement and full expression of love — to the child from the parent, from the child to the parents, and back again in an accentuating circle.

A New Discovery

It is small wonder then that *by the time he is three, every child is deeply, intensely in love with his parents.*

In many instances, this first great love is never excelled in adult life.

Thousands of men and woman fail to find, when grown up, any love-situation to compare with this original one, and remain single, without ever realizing the underlying reason.

"Blind Love"

With every condition ideal and ripe for love on the part of the parent and the child, and with every tradition backing up the parents' love for their children, it is inevitable that parents and children should develop a devotion for each other that is all the more intense because all the rest of the world blocks love. For this very reason it is inevitable that this concentrated love should sometimes subconsciously exceed the bounds of cold reason.

It is always a surprise to outsiders to see the blindness of parental devotion. It is equally surprising, looked at from the standpoint of actual facts, to see the blind faith of the child in his weak or unworthy parents.

But all this is inevitable. We love those who love us. We believe in those who love us, even after we are old enough to know better. So it is hardly to be expected that the young child should refrain from pouring out its instinctive affection upon the parents who

By Elsie Lincoln Benedict and Ralph Paine Benedict

comfort, feed and shelter it and who shower upon it the affections it demands.

Oedipus and Electra

It is true in most cases (for reasons entirely apart from sexual ones) that the daughter loves the father more than she loves the mother, and that the boy loves his mother more than he loves his father.

But that the sexual element predominates even unconsciously in this relationship is as false as it is unfair. And it is proven in this fact: that at least one- third of all girls love their mothers more, while more than a third of all boys love their fathers best. "Oedipus" and "Electra" are indeed myths.

What Determines The Child's Love

Which parent will the child love more? If we need any further proof of the fact that the ego-urge is more powerful than the sex-urge we find it in the answer to this question.

For, the child will love most that parent who most appeals to his ego, regardless of sex.

The child will center its greatest love exactly where the rest of us do — on those who are most devoted to him.

If the father is more strict, more unyielding than the mother the daughter will love her mother best, and the greater warmth of her devotion to her mother will be in proportion to the differences in their treatment of her

For instance, if a father is extremely severe with his children and the mother almost as much so, all the children, regardless of sex, will love their mother more, though not much more than their father.

If she is the opposite extreme from the father — if she gives them their way, pets, loves, fondles and forgives them where he punishes and tyrannizes — all the children will adore their mother and (whether or not they ever admit it even to themselves) subconsciously dislike their father. Regardless of how right he was or how wrong and weak the mother was, this will invariably be true.

107

On the other hand, if the mother is austere, undemonstrative and a hard taskmaster, her children may have great respect for her and consciously admire her more than a worthless father. But if that father indulges them, and shows more affection — though he be a drunkard, thief or murderer — still will all the children love him best.

And they will continue to do so just so long as he is the more indulgent parent.

This love is from the subconscious, and the subconscious, as has been stated before, knows nothing of these modern standards of conduct. It deals with the expression of the individual. It is for whatever and whoever serves his instinctive cravings.

Parental Partiality

The accuracy of all this can be proved at any moment by any person from his own experience.

Regardless of whether he is willing to confess it or not, he knows that the parent he truly feels the greatest affection for is that one who was the more kind, more loving and more indulgent with him. If, as often happens, the severe parent selects one of his children for special favors — if he shows partiality to that child to a greater extent than does the other parent — that particular child will begin to prefer him to the other parent, whereas the recognition of this partiality by the other children will make all the others withdraw farther and farther from the father and nearer to the mother.

Fathers and Daughters

Here we come to the secret back of all the father-daughter and mother-son complexes. And like most secrets it proves upon investigation to be a perfectly simple thing after all!

It is true that most daughters love their fathers best simply and solely *because most fathers indulge their daughters more than they indulge their sons.*

In other words then, because they are conscious of the difference in sex and have been trained to protect women, fathers more often do for their daughters than for their sons the things that inevitably win love from any one at any time under any conditions.

Let a father who has thus won his daughter's love suddenly begin to favor his son while the mother, who has been partial to the son, suddenly commences to show extreme favoritism to the daughter — and both these children, after a few days or weeks of suffering and uncertainty, will interchange their affections and go on just as before with their new loves.

Mothers and Sons

It is true that most sons love their mothers more than they love their fathers and for the same reason as that stated above. *In all such instances the mother has shown more love and indulgence to the son than did the father.*

Here, again, we come to the effect of tradition. Just as the father indulged the daughter because of the traditional protection of women by men, he is inclined to be strict with his son because tradition says sons must be made to stand alone.

But the old subconscious knows naught of these things which have come recently into the world. All the boy's subconscious knows is that he loves his mother best.

His affection for her is enhanced by her devotion to him — a devotion in which she too is the creature of tradition.

Women are expected to minister to males. Her son is a young male, a wee man. To him she naturally and habitually tends to give the best of things, and he inevitably and automatically to love her best.

Love's Tragedy

I All this is delightful to the child. He loves to love and be loved. His childhood is more wonderful by far than that of the children who, for any reason, do not receive this unstinted affection. But he often pays a tremendous price for it in later years.

To, the boy who loves his mother, that mother becomes the epitome, the symbol of all that is desirable in love.

As a man he can love only those women who bear a real or imaginary resemblance to her.

If he can find no woman who seems to him at all like his beloved mother he will never fall in love.

The more superior the mother and the more deeply and exclusively he loved her, the less likelihood will there be of his finding any one resembling her.

Unconscious Love

Proof of how deeply submerged are some of our strongest impulses is seen in the fact that all this is unknown to the individual in whom it is operating so strongly.

He has never been consciously in love with his mother and may even imagine he would prefer women who are very different from her, but the fact remains that those who are different from her never appeal to him, while he will fall in love at first sight with one who recapitulates the mother-symbol.

The daughter who loved her father may never know why she cannot find it in her heart to marry any man. The real reason — that she is unconsciously still in love with her father, or rather with the image of him which she carries in her subconscious — is usually inconceivable to her.

She may care little or nothing for him now. He may be the kind of man whom her mature judgment and lifelong training tell her is beneath her affection; she may know he has always been beneath it; but it will not alter that subconscious symbol.

The man she loves is not her father as he is today, as he looks today, nor is it her father himself *whom* she loves.

Image-Love

What she loves is the *image of him* — face, features, ungrayed hair, smiles, gentleness and all — that he was *in her babyhood days*.

She loves in men only those things which her father seemed to be in that far-off time. She admires only those men who have the traits her father *seemed* to have.

She will never truly love any man who does not, in some or several particulars, remind that subconscious mind of hers of this Father-image.

110

As in the man's case, this woman seldom dreams what it is that determines her attitude toward men. She was not consciously in love with her father, any more than he was consciously in love with his mother.

Love Is Subconscious

"What in the world did he see in her?" and " How did she ever happen to fall in love with him?" are questions the world often asks.

The real answer is never forthcoming because nobody knows it, least of all the person whose taste is being discussed.

Such a man may explain to you for hours at a time the many delightful traits he "saw in her," but the fact of the matter is that what he saw in her was his original love-image.

If as a child he was tenderly cared for and loved by some other woman because of his mother's death or absence, it will be her image as he loved it then which he will seek.

The Subconscious, Unconscious Seeker

In all this it must be borne in mind that the person need not necessarily look like the loved parent, for the reason (as has been stated in earlier lessons) that the subconscious tends to take, not the whole, but a part or section of a thing and let it stand for the total.

There is no knowing what element it will take as the symbol of the whole (much depending, as we saw in the "Emotions" lesson, on the emotional intensity accompanying isolated incidents).

So there is no way of determining, without a mental analysis, either by one's self or an analyst, what characteristic was chosen by the subconscious as the symbol of the loved parent.

A Self-Test

The nearest one can come to knowing what symbolizes this parent in his mind, if he does not already know, or if he cannot be fully analyzed by an expert, is to ask himself this question:

What is the first thing that comes into my mind when I speak the name of my favorite parent?

The difficulty with this question is that, having read this question before putting it to yourself, your conscious mind tends to short-circuit the real answer.

It therefore tends to throw the switch on it, as it were, and deliver the answer in accordance with your conscious preferences, rather than the facts.

But if the question were put to you by an analyst without your knowing its significance, your answer would, under proper conditions, come direct from your subconscious mind

Testing For Preferences

If by any chance you are still in doubt as to which of your parents you loved more you can test yourself by the following:

Which one do I think of first when recalling my parents?

Under an analyst your spontaneous answer to this would be the name of the parent you had loved best.

There are several reasons why it is not easy for us to analyze ourselves, especially in the matters referred to in this lesson.

The first one is that when we know the significance and meaning of the question the surface mind almost invariably intercepts the true answer before it comes to the threshold of consciousness, and substitutes one in keeping with its own standards.

A Pair of Brown Eyes

An illustration of this was seen a short time ago in a woman of middle age who had had a most lonely life. She had been in love but once, and then with a man who was already married.

She criticised herself for years for having cared for another woman's husband, though she had no overt acts to be ashamed of, and in fact had never indicated to the man nor to anyone else that she cared for him.

She left the city where he lived, but worked in uncongenial positions, with uncongenial people and, instead of caring less for him, felt that she was caring more as the years went on.

At last it so happened that this man not only moved to the city where she was but was employed in the same establishment as herself.

She was determined to rid herself of what she had all these years termed her "unholy affection."

She had no real respect for this man, who was mentally and morally her inferior. But his dark brown eyes made her forget everything save her love for him.

Analysis showed that she had really loved her shiftless father because he had been most indulgent to her in her childhood.

As she grew older and realized his mental and moral weaknesses she ceased to respect him and was not really sorry when he passed on.

She lived with and supported her mother who had suffered much at the father's hands.

So fully did she respect her mother's superior qualities that she supposed she cared more for her than she had ever cared for the father.

Two tests brought out the fact that her father had dark brown eyes and that dark brown eyes of a particular expression were to her the symbol not only of her father but of all love.

The similarity of expression in the married man's brown eyes, his shiftlessness, and moral and mental weaknesses, all combined to revive the old symbol.

When fully convinced that it was not the married man she loved but the symbols of which he reminded her, she ceased instantly to care for him.

A Soft Voice

A physician who had struggled for many years with a growing dislike for his wife was analyzed.

He had consciously refused to display this aversion or encourage it. It had assumed such proportions, however, and was arousing such dangerous emotions that he feared not only for his health but for the future of their family

It was found that when he was twenty- eight he had had an accident which it was feared would make him permanently blind.

He spent nine weeks in a hospital with his eyes bandaged.

Long before they were unbandaged he had fallen in love with the waitress who brought the meals to his bedside, though he could not explain why.

When he saw her for the first time he found she did not look at all as he expected her to. But that did not prevent his marrying her two weeks afterward — as soon as they were sure his eyes would be normal again.

Analysis showed that what he had really fallen in love with was the girl's voice. It was low and sweet like that of his mother whom he had subconsciously loved but who had been dead many years. He pictured her face, before he saw it, as that of his mother.

By the time they removed the bandages from his eyes he was so deeply in love with the symbol-voice he forgave the difference in the face.

If the mother's face instead of her voice had been the love-symbol in his mind he would not have loved this girl.

But her face was secondary and thus relinquished, when necessary, from the ensemble.

The mother's voice was the real symbol of love to him and any woman with this voice would have appealed to him.

Before he had been married a week he realized that this woman's voice was the only thing she possessed in common with his beloved mother. The wife was, in fact, the almost exact opposite of the mother, most of whose traits he unconsciously loved.

Their marriage had been to him one disillusionment after another. His wife was unlearned where his mother had been highly educated. She was uncouth and crude where his mother had been refined; rough, outspoken and quarrelsome, where the mother had been amiability and gentility itself.

He tried to accustom himself to her, to overlook, to convince himself that this woman who loved him and bore his children was not to blame. He had been brought up to believe that a husband and father had no right, under any circumstances, to think of himself; that his family deserved his time, strength and love, regardless of everything.

To escape from the hated reality he drank much coffee, then other stimulants, and when we met him had been taking drugs some time.

It was very difficult for this man who had treated others for so long in his practice to relax sufficiently and confide sufficiently to the analyst to give her the story of the real (though hitherto unrealized reason) for his falling in love with this woman so far beneath him.

It was not easy for him to admit that things medicine could not touch could be brought out into the sunlight and cured by mental analysis. But such was the case.

He was shown the exact facts — that he had not turned away from his wife for the reason that he had never loved her.

He had married what he supposed was a woman like his mother and she was utterly different.

His years of brave struggle to keep from hurting her — a large husky woman — had resulted in almost wrecking his own much more refined organism.

A recognition of the facts and the restoration of his self-respect enabled him within a few months to resume his practice and give up his drug habit.

The Brownings

This love between mothers and sons and fathers and daughters, with its far-flung influence upon human lives, is seen in almost every great love of history.

But nowhere is it more strikingly illustrated than in that most illustrious love- union of modern times — between Elizabeth Barrett and Robert Browning.

We will quote direct from its sympathetic and poetic raconteur, Elbert Hubbard, in his "Little Journeys:"

"Robert Browning's mother was a woman of fine feeling and much poetic insight. She knew good books. The mother and son moused in books together and, according to Mrs. Sutherland Orr, his biographer, this love of mother and son took upon itself the nature of a passion.

"She was an invalid Shut-In, reclining always on a couch.

"The love of Robert Browning for Elizabeth Barrett was a revival and a renewal of the condition of tenderness and sympathy that existed between Browning and his mother.

"There certainly was a strange and marked resemblance in the characters of Elizabeth Barrett and the mother of Robert Browning; and to many this fully accounts for the instant affection that Browning felt toward the occupant of the 'darkened room.' when first they met.

"It also accounts for the answering love Elizabeth Barrett gave him that first moment. Robert Browning was, on first sight, much more the father-type than the poet. His frame was compact and strong — *like her father's*. His poise, his protective power symbolized the things her father had meant to her in her childhood days when he was all love for her.

"Edward Barrett had a sort of fierce, passionate, jealous affection for his daughter Elizabeth. He set himself the task of educating her from her very babyhood. He was her constant companion, her tutor, adviser, friend.

"The child's health broke. From her thirteenth year she appears to us like a beautiful spirit.

"But she did not much complain. She had a will as strong as her father's, and felt a Spartan pride in doing all the studying he asked and a little more. She read, translated, thought.

"To spur her on and to stimulate her, he published several volumes of her poems.

" Came a time when Mr. Barrett was jealous of his daughter — of the fame that was taking her away from him. The passion of father for daughter, of mother for son — there is often something lover-like in it — a deal of whimsy!

"Edward Barrett's daughter — she of the raven curls and gentle ways — was reaching a point where her father's love was not her life.

"A good way to drive love away is to be jealous. He had seen it coming years before; he had brooded over it ; the calamity was upon him. Her fame was growing; someone called her the Shakespeare of women.

By Elsie Lincoln Benedict and Ralph Paine Benedict

"Edward Barrett scowled. He accused her foolishly and falsely of perverseness. He attempted to dictate to her — she must use this ink or that. Why? Because he said so. He quarreled with her to ease the love-hurt that was smarting in his heart.

"Mr. Browning, who had heard of Miss Barrett and admired her work, wrote asking permission to call upon her.

"Miss Barrett replied that her father would not allow it, neither would the doctor or nurse; that she lived in a darkened room. She added, 'There is nothing to see in me.'

"But this repulse only made Mr. Browning want to see her the more. He appealed to her cousin, an elderly gentleman who was the only person allowed to call.

"The cousin arranged it. He timed the hour when Mr. Barrett was down town, and the nurse and doctor safely out of the way, and they called on the invalid prisoner in the darkened room.

"They did not stay long, but when they went away Robert Browning trod on air. The beautiful girl-like face, in its frame of dark curls, lying back among the pillows, haunted him like a shadow. She was slipping away. He would love her back to life and light!

"And so Robert Browning told her all this shortly afterward......

"She grew better.

"And soon we find her getting up and throwing wide the shutters. It was no longer a darkened room. The sunlight came dancing through the windows.

"The doctor was indignant; the nurse resigned. Of course Mr. Barrett was not taken into confidence, and no one asked his consent. Why should they? She was thirty-five — and her father a man who could never understand.

"So one fine day when the coast was clear, the couple went over to Saint Marylebone Church and were married. The bride went home alone — could walk all right now — and it was a week before her husband saw her, because he would not be a hypocrite and go ring the doorbell and ask if Miss Barrett was home; and of course if he had asked for Mrs. Robert Browning, no one would have known whom he wanted to see.

117

"But at the end of a week the bride stole down the stairs while the family was at dinner and met her lover-husband there on the street corner where the mail-box is. No one missed the runaways until the next day, and then the bride and groom were safely in France, writing letters back asking forgiveness and blessings ....

"Health came back, and joy and peace and perfect love were theirs. But it was joy bought with a price — Elizabeth Barrett Browning had forfeited the love of her father. Her letters written to him came back unopened.....He declared she was dead.......

"We regret that this man, so strong and manly in many ways, could not be reconciled to this exalted love.

"Why could he not have followed the example of John Kenyon who had always loved her and who, it is said, did not smile for two years after her elopement?".....

The answer is to be found in human psychology which today shows us that many who *think* they love someone are really only loving themselves!

When you truly love you want the adored one to have not *you* necessarily but whatever he or she desires.

That John Kenyon truly loved Elizabeth Barrett was proven when in his will he left all he had — fifty thousand dollars — to the Brownings, to add the last touch to their happiness.

They were poor but his kindness placed them forever beyond financial-fear and gave them perfect peace.

Sex vs. Love

In this ideal mating of the Brownings, as in all great loves, it was again proved that it is love rather than sex which most human beings seek in marriage.

People seek marriage *in proportion as they lack love and friendship in their lives.*

Many a handsome bachelor remains unmarried not because women do not care for him but precisely because they *do.*

This satisfies his demand for love without the entanglements resultant from wedlock.

Psychology also explains why, at fifty or so, these men finally marry. They are beginning to lose their attractiveness, the love and friendships of women which have substituted for marriage became fewer in number and fainter in feeling.

Such a man awakens to the fact that if he is to be supplied with personal affection he must find a mate and "settle down."

Truth About Bachelors

While it is true that many supposedly celibate men and women live far different lives from what we imagine, it is equally true that the attractive, popular type of bachelor described usually lives a far more celibate life than the sophisticated would believe.

We base this statement not only upon observation and knowledge of psychology, but upon our experience with thousands of students throughout the United States.

Many of these men have stated in private analyses (where they can be even more frank than with their physician, and where there is the fullest understanding and consequent tolerance of every human weakness) that though they bore the reputation of being exceedingly gay[3], as a matter of fact they lived lives of chastity *out of preference.*

Many of these men desired an analysis largely to find why they preferred to live this life instead of the one popularly ascribed to them — the kind they also supposed other such men lived.

In many instances such a man has labored under the delusion that he was "queer,[4]" " freakish" or abnormal, and was relieved but not surprised when he learned that his was not only a perfectly normal but much more prevalent attitude than the world realizes.

It is not the popular man but the unpopular one (who gets little or no love from anyone) who seeks sexual expression and who, instead of the celibate life credited to him, lives one containing sexual experiences that would amaze his unsuspecting friends.

The Flirtatious Woman

The same is true of the flirtatious, attractive woman — and especially of the supposedly dangerous young widow.

---

[3] When this book was written, the slang "gay" did not have the same meaning as today.

[4] Again, the slang word "queer"'s meaning has evolved over time.

It cannot be repeated too often that what the human being desires most is *not* sex but *love.* If love of a personal nature can be obtained without sex many there are, in both sexes, who much prefer single blessedness to mating, and celibacy to sexual expression.

The attractive woman who can win and hold the devotion, attention, affection and love of men — to whom they send flowers, candy, books and other gifts — is never the sexual creature she is painted.

This also we know from private analyses of thousands of such women. The adulation which the ego is always subconsciously craving in love is satisfied by these attentions. The love-demand is met by the affections of a large number of men. Often they feel no further need of expression.

The Female Puritan

It is the quiet, self-effacing, timid, plain and outwardly puritanical woman who dwells on the matters of sex, searches the libraries for sex literature and finds sexual expression in the least-suspected paths.

She it is also who is most easily induced to give herself out of wedlock because her heart is so starved for love.

Such a woman, if no longer young, or if of the extremely repressed type, often refuses, but it is in the face of terrific struggle.

She desires *not* to refuse, more than the self-expressive woman can ever know. Her will power deserves our utmost respect.

The Real Unsexuality of Love

All these and myriads of corroborative situations, facts and conditions throughout all human experience prove conclusively that even *love is far less crassly sexual than we have ever supposed.*

Every human being craves understanding, communion and the certainty of intimate personal interest.

We believe the time will come when all thinking men and women will recognize that *the things of sex are resorted to not so much for their own sake as because they give the surest and completest sense of this deep personal intimacy.*

120

By Elsie Lincoln Benedict and Ralph Paine Benedict

Look in any direction you will, under any condition, observe any person or persons of any race, nationality, education, belief or training, and you will find what historians have always seen but never understood — that the instant this personal intimacy is fully established the sexual element assumes a less important role.

Once the sexual act has taken place the utmost intimacy known to humans is established. The sex urge is, to a far greater degree than we have ever dreamed, merely a means to this end.

Having fulfilled its mission it immediately takes a secondary place. This again proves to us how much more of the ego element exists in even the wildest love than we have ever recognized.*[5]

The Passing of Passion

Hundreds of women and men wonder why no subsequent sexual experience with the same mate ever rises to the heights of the first. Many whose mates love them more than they did at first, imagine that because passion has died, love has flown.

The exact opposite is more often true.

Passion is always and invariably self- centered, egoistic and wholly *self-expressive*. It cannot, by its very nature, awaken or exist minus these qualities — any more than you can become hungry because another has been without food, nor halt your own starvation by watching him eat.

To yield one's self without desire as the instrument of another's desire, is unselfish (though a most dangerous and reprehensible kind of unselfishness!) — but to satisfy one's own desire is the essence and epitome of self- seeking.

An Old Mystery Solved

Many a wife and many a husband who recognizes this subconsciously withdraws from contact with his mate for no other reason than his aversion to being made merely an avenue of self-expression for another.

This again illustrates the all-pervading urge of the ego.

---

[5] *For further elaboration of the ego instinct see "The Human Instincts" by Elsie Lincoln Benedict and Ralph Paine Benedict.

121

The greater the ego of such a one the more certain is he to retreat from his mate when his subconscious finally becomes aware of the facts.

He may never suspect the reason for the cooling of his ardor. On the other hand it may be a fully conscious reaction.

Sex and Complexes

If he has reached the age or stage of life when the sexual urge is less dominant this withdrawal and relinquishment of sexual expression may have no appreciable effect.

But if such a one still loves his or her mate and is still very much alive sexually, there may arise a conflict between the ego instinct on one hand (which refuses to adapt itself to utilization by another) and the sex instinct (which demands expression and knows nothing save its own desires).

In these cases — and there are tens of thousands of them — conflicts and complexes of various kinds arise — always in accordance with the type of the individual.

As time goes on and one finds that his mate bears little or no resemblance to his ideal-image, he will try to forget, or fight his aversion; seek new relationships or separate — depending again upon his type and temperament.

For You

If you were one of a large family of children the probabilities are you did not have enough parent-love lavished on you exclusively to establish a too-vivid love-image.

If you were brought up by someone other than your parents it is not likely that you were harmed by a too-intense affection.

If you grew up in an institution you doubtless received too little love and were permitted to show too little.

But in any case, this lesson cannot fail to help you.

Read it carefully, be frank with yourself. Through it you will come ultimately to a deeper understanding of your own personal problems.

By Elsie Lincoln Benedict and Ralph Paine Benedict

Why build these cities glorious
If MAN unbuilded goes?
In vain we build the world unless
The builder also grows.
We all are blind until we see
That in the human plan
Nothing is worth the making
If it does not make the man.

— Edwin Markham

Lesson VI
Success Through The Subconscious

Success is, next to love, the most vital matter in one's life, for only through successful accomplishment of some nature can civilized men and women be thoroughly happy.

Not only does success fulfil a great personal need by aiding in the self-expression of the individual but through it he contributes to the progress of the world.

These two elements are necessary to the happiness of any normal man or woman.

First, the normal individual desires self- expression. But a close second is his sincere desire to help humanity. The latter is not a mere margin which he wishes to dispose of but a natural demand of his "success instinct."

Civilized man has two roles and is taught early in life what they are. He is himself — and himself is ever his primary consideration. But he is also a part of society — a tiny section in a great mosaic.

The average individual thinks chiefly of that little self-section — not so much because he is selfish or narrow but because his own troubles, problems and difficulties are so great he has little time, energy or thought left over to give to the general pattern.

The greatest result of Mental Analysis is that it is helping the individual to untangle his own troubles.

The moment this is done the rest follows. He awakens to the needs of his fellows — his family's first, then his friends', next his acquaintances', and in time, the world's.

Life at Loose Ends

Many more lives than we realize are ruined from a lack of definite connection with the world of real work.

The individual himself (and especially if it be a herself) often wonders what is wrong and goes through years or a lifetime without realizing that it is the thwarting of this natural success instinct which is causing the difficulty.

125

Three Classes

If his supreme wish is to spend his life in some particular kind of activity, regardless of its tasks or drudgeries, and if he concentrates on this activity, he will become a genius. But if his choice of a vocation is secondary to his wish — that is, if it is selected only as an adjunct to the wish — an aid and abettor of something he desires more — and he gets into such a vocation, he will be in it only one of the many big successes.

If he spends his life in a kind of work which calls for traits which he has only in a small degree, he will be mediocre.

If his work demands activities that are the opposite of his natural ones he will be a failure.

The Subconscious Sentinel

In each case the subconscious mind registers feelings for or against certain vocations and for or against specific lines of work contemplated by the individual.

Your preference for or prejudice against any line of work is not an accident nor a mystery. It is an emotion based in the subconscious unreasoning feeling that this vocation would help or hinder the materialization of your supreme wish.

It automatically votes against everything which would interfere with your life's desires and for everything of any nature (including vocation) that aids and abets them.

The Genius

The child destined to become a genius has, like every other, a supreme subconscious wish. But this wish differs from that of the average child in two things — *intensity and content.*

The supreme subconscious wish of the vast majority of men, women and children is *to possess things.*

The supreme wish of the genius-child is to *do a certain kind of thing.*

The average supreme wish, though it may be fired with the deepest emotion of which that individual is capable, is much less intense and furious than that of the genius-child.

126

These two lead to the third element — opportunity — as inevitably as the desire and ability to sing point the song bird instinctively to an opportunity to unburden his silvery throat.

Requisites of Genius

So we find that the requisites for the making of a genius are:

1. A desire to *do a certain kind of thing*, regardless of good or bad consequences.

2. That this desire shall constitute the *one supreme, subconscious wish* of his life, in comparison with which all else is insignificant.

3. That this *supreme wish to do a certain kind of thing* shall be so *intense* as to allow no room for feelings of doubt.

These things and these only have invariably differentiated the genius from other men and women.

These intense inner urges *compel* the genius to find opportunity for doing the thing he wants to do. He has no peace until he does it. Once started at it, satisfaction permeates his spirit, saturates his soul. He is at the business for which he was created; he has found himself.

Finding Himself (or Herself)

In this supremest of human achievements — meeting and working with one's self face to face — the genius forgets all else.

Is it to be wondered at that such enthusiasm produces great things?

Other men give but a fraction of themselves to their work and none of their subconscious selves to work they dislike. The subconscious of the genius is in tune with the world.

Any man who *wants* to do a thing with the same intensity, the same selfless, concentrated determination can make of himself a genius.

But the average man does not want to *do*; he only wants to *have without doing.*

He is always expecting to " put one over" on Fate.

It can't be done.

Are You a Genius ?

"A genius is one who cannot be kept away from his work." If nothing can keep you away from yours, if you love its toil and drudgery so much it is play, this means that to do this thing is your supreme subconscious wish. Whatever you supremely, subconsciously wish can and does come true, as you will see in the last lesson of this course.

The Successful

Those who are not geniuses but the next- highest — the big successes in any line — are those whose supreme wish is to *achieve a certain goal* and *who are willing to do any- thing honorable to reach it*, no matter how hard, how humiliating or how difficult the necessary sacrifices.

Such a man or woman will become ultimately a supreme success. For him, as for the genius, there is no question of opportunity. The world is full of opportunity and he knows it. Such a man says

"With doubt and dismay you are smitten?
You think there's no chance for you, son?
Why, the best books haven't been written,
The chances have only begun;
The best score hasn't been made yet,
The best race hasn't been run.
The best game hasn't been played yet,
Cheer up, for the world is young!"

The trouble with the unsuccessful is not that they lack ability or opportunity. They lack none of the success-requisites save one, and that one they can get any moment they want it — willingness to *pay the price.*

Why They Make Money

We can apply the one big secret of their success to higher ones. That secret is the one stated above — a willingness to make any sacrifice necessary to success in a chosen undertaking.

128

This type of person — regardless of race, color, nationality, training, education or environment — is bound to win. He can bear any humiliation and make any sacrifice for success.

One Thing

A woman who has attained fame and fortune by her own efforts, despite poverty, ill health, ugliness and other handicaps, was talking not long ago to a small group of old friends whom she had not seen since she was a ragged little girl in the ragged little Western town where she grew up.

"Let me see, Helen, didn't you wait table once at the Smith Central? I seem to remember seeing you there when you were about fifteen," asked one of the friends.

"Yes," she replied, " and the Summer before that I washed dishes at the Belvedere, and the Summer before that I had a strenuous position as cook, scrub woman and maid-of-all-work on a big ranch where forty men were employed. The rancher's wife had a nap every afternoon and retired at nine. I was up at five and did not sit down from that time until midnight.

"But I had a wonderful time. I needed that $3 a week to buy books and clothes for high school that Fall. When Fall came I got another job — working for my board in a family of seven children — but I had to have an education and thought I was a lucky girl to even *get* a job!"

After more mutual reminiscences one of the women turned to the now successful one and said, " Did you ever select anything and say you would not do that — didn't you have powerful aversions to doing some things?"

" There was one," the woman replied — "just one thing I always said even as a child that I would not do. I said it over and over, and it was, ' I will *not* fail!'"

Flirting With Failure

If you care enough about being a success to stop flirting with failure you will find the work and the opportunities necessary to make you one.

People miss success because they want to eat their cake and have it too. They won't do this and they are too good to do that; they are above this and superior to that — in their youth. At middle age they are making excuses, and at sixty many are brought to to a choice between those very same menial things and the poorhouse.

False pride has cheated more people out of success than any other thing in this world.

Pride that is *real* is too proud to drag you a frazzled failure through this world of opportunity!

Self-Tests for Success

The content of your own subconsciousness determines your success or failure.

To know whether you are going to be a real success you have but to ask yourself the following questions:

1. Which of these two attitudes predominate in my mind : the determination *against* doing certain things or a determination to *do* certain things?

2. Do I keep my mental eyes fastened on the *fears of failure* or the *certainties of success?*

3. Do I think more about the obstructions in my pathway — my troubles, my enemies, my handicaps, my disadvantages, my weaknesses — than the *goal* I hope to reach?

The answer to these questions reveals the content of your subconscious as regards success-qualities. If you are wasting your strength *against* things, people, problems and life in general instead of expending it *for* the things you desire, you are running your car in reverse and backing yourself downhill.

Faith or Fear?

If your mind has more fear than faith in it you are going to lose! Nothing on earth can make any man a winner who doesn't believe in himself.

Nothing can make you a failure save yourself.

If your subconscious is centered more on thoughts about your troubles; if your talk is full of them, you will have lots more of them, for you are putting into operation a great law and the law, being immutable, will bring them to you.

Forget Your Enemies

If you burn the candles of memory at the shrine of your enemies you are going to make more enemies and further embitter the ones you already have.

If you think and talk and act out your handicaps, your disadvantages, your weaknesses, you are planting tares and will reap bigger and bigger harvests of these very things as life goes on.

For *your subconscious content makes or mars your life. If it is destructive your life will be destructive.* There is no way on earth to avoid it, though millions have tricked themselves into thinking they could.

The Might of Mind

What is in your mind comes out in your life. You can't fool the Force that rules the universe. That Force decrees that certain causes bring certain results and they always do.

The world calls the successful man an egoist and he is. But he is seldom a vain egotist. He believes in his own strength and proves he has it.

The mediocre and the failures *become* mediocre and fail because they so overrate themselves as to imagine they can outwit divinity. This is not true of every failure but of most.

The Failure Ego

You can apply another little test that will tell you whether any man is this type or not. If he is forever expressing envy, jealousy, suspicion and criticism of the successful it has but one cause — the resentment of his own disappointed ego.

Those who have failed through little fault of their own are never embittered by the successes of others.

If you are constantly deriding, pulling down, carping at the good fortune of others; if you call every successful person vain, selfish or a money-grabber, wake up to yourself.

Realize that this attitude betrays you to every person who knows anything at all about human psychology. It tells him you are only judging others by yourself and that you are assuming they must be all these because your wounded vanity demands consolation.

Self-Revealers

Furthermore, it is a well-known fact that the motives you are in the habit of ascribing to others are what you know your own would be *in their place.* If you cannot see a man successful without calling him vain, it is because you would be vain in his place.

If you cannot see a rich man without calling him mercenary, it is because you are mercenary. If you cannot see another on the pinnacle of fame or fortune without thinking he is insincere it is because *you* lack sincerity.

Subconscious Content

All these are indications of your subconscious content.

Since your subconscious content determines your success, do you not see why some people have failed? People who worked and slaved and skimped — yes, and went to church

You have got to have the pure air of right attitudes blowing through your mental windows if you want to be successful. Andre Tridon says, "The genius is always unselfish. In the neurotic, egotism is a mask for a sense of inferiority."

He and scores of other mental scientists declare that the successful are less vain, less selfish, less deceitful, less mercenary than the failures.

Success and Constructiveness

But that is not by any manner of means the most important thing upon which they agree.

They have found that it is chiefly *because of their more constructive mental attitudes that these people have succeeded.*

Does this not contain a great lesson for every human being? And does it not prove, after all, that regardless of our particular belief or unbelief, the truth was spoken when it was said, " The letter of the law killeth but the spirit maketh alive?"

Your Subconscious Army

Your subconscious is a great standing army you personally own and control.

Through your conscious mind you are giving it orders every waking moment.

If you keep your mind full of destructive thoughts of any nature whatever you are giving destructive orders to your army and it will bring to pass in your life the destructive things you order.

If you have been getting what you did not want it was because, unknowingly, you have been giving your subconscious powers the wrong kind of orders.

Function of the Subconscious

Your subconscious is wrapped and woven around and over and under and through just one thing — your supreme life wish.

It has no function save to see that wish gratified; it never tires, never sleeps, never forgets.

It never accepts excuses; never takes No for an answer; never for so much as an instant lessens its concentration on the attainment of your one supreme aim.

It gathers from every source within your reach all manner of materials for your use in the furthering of this wish, much of which you never suspect until you start to do the thing you want to do.

How the Subconscious Helps

A man has a deep desire for many years to write a certain book. He is so busy with his everyday affairs it is years before he sits down to start the manuscript. He thinks he has only enough material for a beginning.

But he soon finds that through his intense and genuine interest in this subject, his subconscious has gathered data for a dozen books — and hands it out to him.

He is amazed to discover how deeply he has thought on this subject and how many illustrations he has at his tongue's end. He cannot write fast enough to keep up with his mind, which is bursting with material for the tangible products.

But if this man, instead of *deeply desiring* for years to write a book only thinks for years that it would be a good idea to write a book, he will find when he sits down that he has almost no material.

He will awaken to the realization that he knows very little about the subject and that what he does know is unorganized, chaotic and distasteful.

When one truly *desires* to write on a certain subject he has so much material in his mind he scarcely uses his notes. But when he attempts to write anything against his desires he gets little from even the most voluminous notes, memoranda or previous manuscript.

These facts and similar ones are known to every person who tries to do anything he has long desired to do.

Another Test

The condition of your subconscious tells, with unmistakable certainty, whether you are achieving about what you are capable of, whether you are lagging behind or falling far short of what you have the ability to accomplish.

You can go far toward determining for yourself which you are doing by the following tests:

First of all, *in what are you dissatisfied with yourself?*

And, *in what way are you constantly conscious of not coming up to your standards?*

That standard comes from your subconscious and comes because you are capable of doing the very thing you desire to do.

Regret a Recorder

Subconscious discontent is the method taken by your subconscious to register its disapproval. It never disapproves of you for not doing what you *cannot* do. The fact that you regret not living up to a certain ideal is the proof that you are fully able to do so.

The man who can do wrong, weak things without regret is always a far lower-grade man than the one who suffers remorse.

By Elsie Lincoln Benedict and Ralph Paine Benedict

The one who knows the keenest suffering and self- discontent is the man who is possessed of the highest powers.

Ambition — The Acid Test

What is the amount of your ambition?

If you have little it is because you have little ability.

Ambition to do a thing comes from *the capacity to do it and is the demand of that capacity to be brought out and utilized.*

A thing you have no ambition to do you have no ability to do. The man who, at thirty, has no ambition to be an architect will never be an architect.

The woman who, at thirty, has no ambition whatever to sing has no singing ability.

The Real Difference

In this connection do not confuse the kind of work you *really wish to do* with the kind of work you imagine would bring you *the things you want.*

For instance, if you really *want* to sing, for the sheer love of singing and not for its rewards or the things it would bring, you have singing ability.

But if the real desire in the bottom of your subconscious mind is not to *do the singing for the sheer joy of doing it* but to have *the emoluments, honors, glory, fame or money* you think it would produce for you, you have little and perhaps no singing ability.

You will never succeed supremely in any line of work or endeavor which you do not truly, deeply, subconsciously, intensely want to do.

What you want to do you have immeasurable power to do — and the power is in proportion to the *desire.*

The "Sleep Test"

Science has made one other amazing and illuminating discovery. It is that we *crave sleep in proportion as we are unhappy, unhealthy or unsuccessful.*

When we are happy, well, and successful we can stay in perfect health on much less sleep than we require at other times.

When we are disappointed, discouraged, depressed, ill or humiliated we want to escape from reality, and the subconscious furnishes the sleepiness necessary to bring temporary peace.

Napoleon's Sleep

Napoleon required sleep wholly according to whether he was winning or losing battles. Three hours were sufficient when things were going well with him.

His biographers and all historians of the period agree that immediately following his most successful battles he often went several days and nights without any sleep whatever.

After his exile — when the light had gone out for him forever, and he knew it — he slept from ten to fourteen hours out of every twenty-four.

Another Notable Example

t is no mystery either to himself or to the psychologists why Thomas A. Edison requires less than four hours' sleep out of each twenty-four.

He is doing what he *wants* to do. He is achieving in real life, the things his subconscious self, his real self, desires. He is living life to the full.

His conscious and subconscious minds are working in harmony, aiding and abetting each other as they were created to do. There are almost none of the conflicts, interferences, oppositions, misunderstandings, or warfare which split and disintegrate the conscious and subconscious minds of the average individual.

This fact accounts not only for the success of Edison but for that of every successful person who ever lived.

Unlock Your Nine-Tenths

No man can succeed through his conscious mind alone, for this conscious mind is so recent an acquisition in human evolution that it is not yet in good running order. The slightest thing sidetracks it.

Though far more powerful than we have ever suspected, the conscious mind is incapable of the deep concentrated activity of the

136

subconscious. It is flighty, erratic, whimsical, superficial compared to the subconscious mind

The man who puts only his conscious mind on a thing gets only surface results.

The saving fact here, however, is that the man who constantly turns his conscious mind on anything secures the cooperation of his subconscious also — and secures it to whatever degree this thing on which he centers his mind *promises to fulfill the supreme subconscious wish.*

In Your Own Case

For instance, you may consciously dislike to be a traveling salesman. You don't like the traveling, the constant absence from home and friends which it necessitates. But you can do them all provided your supreme subconscious wish is to be the star salesman in your district.

If your supreme wish is not for anything of this kind; especially if your deepest wish is to succeed at something entirely different, you will never get the co-operation of your subconscious mind in your salesmanship, no matter how long you keep at it nor how hard you try.

And all the years you keep at salesmanship you will find relief whenever possible in some form of forgetfulness.

Sleep and the "Sleave of Care"

The safest and sanest of these forms of forgetfulness is our friend Sleep — who "knits up the raveled sleave of care" and tries, by giving the stage of the mind over to the subconscious manager, to further our supreme ambitions.

It takes the teamwork of conscious and subconscious minds, working in harmony both in sleep and in waking hours, to achieve anything great in life. If we sleep too much we hold back the other very necessary part of the team — the conscious mind.

Sleep as the Refuge

As explained in the lesson on "Mental Miracles," whenever you are in trouble of any kind you tend to relieve the conscious mind of the strain — to "lose consciousness." Some types find this relief in long nights of sleep or frequent "naps."

Others seek it in various kinds of drink— the same types invariably choosing drinks furnishing the same kind of reaction. Others seek forgetfulness in excitement, entertainment, society, travel, and the hundreds of other modern allurements.

Any person's craving for these various "aids to forgetfulness" is in proportion to the degree that reality, actuality — the facts of life — are disappointing or disillusioning him.

Desire For Drugs

Thus the man who is discharged, jilted, financially ruined or worried, takes to drink if he is of a certain type.

If he is of another type this same disappointment turns him toward the deep oblivion brought by drugs — in which case he will again choose the particular kind of drug that appeals to his particular temperament. Every suicide is committed in the effort to escape reality. The fact that the rich, beautiful and apparently happy destroy themselves shows how little we know of the inner facts of any other human being's life.

That "dope" and drug "fiends" are often sensitive, keenly intellectual and idealistic individuals is not accidental. Such organisms, for a combination of reasons, find the harshness of reality too awful to bear.

For these reasons we are short-sighted and narrow when we blame or despise the person who resorts to any of these things. He is in trouble. What he needs and deserves is our sympathy and understanding.

Success and Sleep

Success, as each individual sees it, comes from the materialization of his supreme subconscious wish. The man who makes a million but who has missed the one big thing he wanted does not consider himself successful; but the one who wanted only to make money says when he does it, "I have succeeded."

Success is, after all, a matter of personal viewpoint. You may not know what any given individual's standard of success or happiness is, but there is one way in which you can tell with absolute certainty whether he is coming up to the standard he has set for himself, and that is by noting how much or how little of his time he gives to things that bring mental oblivion.

The man who is achieving his supreme subconscious wish is so happy in the realization of life that he feels little need of any kind of mental oblivion.

Sleep An Instinct

Facts gathered over large areas and through long periods of time concerning the life of men and women in all countries in all ages show that sleep is an instinct, just as is eating or sex, and that it is resorted to, as are other instincts, in the degree as other instincts are undeveloped or unexpressed.

Because sleep makes us harmless instead of harmful as some of the other instincts do, society has smiled upon it and encouraged it — unless it is carried to excess — in which case society (feeling itself endangered by it) will criticize it, and apply the much-feared appellation "lazy" to whoever over-indulges in it.

Carried to excess, sleep is as reprehensible as the excessive expression of any other instinct, but deserves more consideration at our hands even in its excess than we have been inclined to give, for no individual anesthetizes his senses save when those senses are suffering.

Sleep In Future Ages[6]

As man learns more and more how to coordinate his two minds he will be more and more successful and happy.

As more and more men and women emulate in their lives the perfect co-ordination of powers seen in Edison they will more and more emulate his four hours of sleep. And, ages hence, when we have learned how to live, the instinct of withdrawal from reality (which came down to us from the ages when reality was almost unbearable) will fade away.

---

[6] We know today that 7 to 8 hours of sleep; or more for children and teens, is essential to physical and mental health.

When that time comes there will be no beds, no skyscrapers honeycombed with "bedrooms" in which living men retire for hours from reality — and we will use constructively the *third of our lifetime* which we now spend in sleep.

Success and Your Subconscious

Will you make a success of your job?

The answer to this big question must have dawned on you while you have been reading this lesson. At least it has given you such insights into the real reasons for your own successes and failures as you never had before.

It must be clear to you now that the things at which you failed were things which, for some reason, lacked the complete cooperation of your subterranean, subconscious forces. It is these things and not just hard work that make any undertaking a success

It must be equally clear to you why your own triumphs and those of other people often came from less work than you had devoted to the thing that failed.

You now know why, in the moment of winning, you could scarcely realize that the winner was really you.

You also know why you often felt you really didn't deserve such a lot of credit as people gave you; that the person who did this successful thing was not you but someone working through you — someone bigger and stronger than yourself.

Will You Succeed ?

But to get back to the big question — will you succeed ?

You will succeed provided your supreme subconscious wish is for success. If your deepest, most absorbing desire is for success nothing under Heaven can keep it from you.

If your supreme wish is for something else than success you will get that something else. If it is for mediocre success you will achieve mediocre success. If it is for supreme, sublime success you will get it.

You will get it because it would then be your supreme, subconscious wish.

How that wish is to be attained will be made clear in the next lesson — a lesson containing hitherto unpublished and until very recently unknown laws of the most vital import to every human being.

The high soul goes the. high way
And the low soul gropes the low,
While in between on the misty flats.
The rest drift to and fro.

But to every man there openeth
A high way and a low.
And every man decideth
Which way his soul shall go.

— John Oxenham.

Lesson VII
How To Attain Your Supreme Wish

What, more than anything else in the world, do *you* want out of life?

The answer you make, in your secret soul, to this question determines with utter, inexorable certainty *what you are going to get.* Not the details — they don't count — but ultimately, eventually in *your life as a whole.*

In this lesson is published, for the first time, the most recent and by far the most startling psychological discovery concerning the real secret of human happiness that has been made in the history of scientific research.

It will show you to your complete satisfaction what has been holding you back and how to take your foot off the brake if you really desire to do so.

It is going to take the props from under some of your pet alibis, but if you are the honest seeker after truth which your study of mental analysis implies, you will be glad to part with them in return for the great self-revelation and self-realization this lesson gives you.

Why You Lost

This lesson will show you, with intense clarity, why you have lost many things you tried to get. It will show you where the fault lay and where it came from. It will show you who was to blame and why. It will show you how that person was to blame for your not accomplishing the thing you attempted. It will show you exactly what stood in your path and who put it there. It will show you how to take obstructions away from your path in future if you really desire to be free of them. It will also show you why and how others have failed.

Why You Won

This lesson will show you why you succeeded when you did succeed.

It will show you why you seemed to do the biggest things most easily; why you had, through it all, a sense of not really doing it yourself but of being the instrument, as it were, of a person bigger and stronger than yourself.

It will show you why you lived through some of your greatest tragedies in spite of the conviction that you never would.

It shows you the real, inner secret of all your own accomplishments and those of other people.

It shows you the great law which has brought every personal success, every personal achievement and every personal triumph that has ever been accomplished in this world.

Why You Did Them

It shows you why you always find time, strength and opportunity to do certain things and none for certain others; why you "give up" certain ambitions and reconcile your- self to going without all kinds of things you had supposed paramount in your life while clinging tenaciously to others which your common sense tells you are inconsequential.

It shows you why the people of the supposedly greatest gifts fail while others, who started with few, go to the top of Life's Ladder.

It shows you why you have permitted some of your own greatest talents to lie undeveloped while working hard to succeed at something for which you seem to have no ability.

Clues To Our Own Mysteries

You have sometimes wondered why you simply could not go on with a thing which you knew was for your own best good. You have marveled at your capacity for making the *same kind* of mistake over and over.

You have become disgusted and often discouraged with yourself for the inexplicable reactions certain things and especially certain work cause in you.

You have thought of all these and a thousand other self-mysteries, and either arrived at some theory that appeals to your particular type and temperament, or you have given it up, thinking — and perhaps saying — " There is no accounting for us; a human being is a conglomeration of enigmas! "

Life a Mystifying Drama

The average individual is like a child seeing a moving picture for the first time. He sees an amazing, mystifying, myriad -sectioned drama unwind before his eyes. To him it is the realest of reality. All is as it seems on the screen — and all arises from and returns to the unseen, the mysterious.

The average unthinking individual lives in a maze of moving mysteries which he calls his life. The unexpected is always happening to him. The expected and longed-for happens but seldom and when it does he cannot see how nor why, so is unable, in any way, to repeat it.

He no more attempts to understand the laws back of his life-dream than the three- year-old child at the movies attempts to figure out how pictures are made. He swallows it, enjoys what he can, registers verbal disapproval when things go wrong — but *sits and takes it*, like the babe in the theater

He feels helpless, often hopeless. But it is too big a tangle to understand or straighten out; so there he waits watching his life-story play itself out as it will.

Making Your Own Movies

This lesson is to prove to you that your life-movie doesn't " just happen;" that you are not at the mercy of Fate; that *you* and *you alone* make your own life drama.

It is going to show you that the play in which you are acting the life-picture you see unwinding before your eyes each day, is based on laws as sane, simple and scientific as those back of the making of a motion picture. It is going to do for you, in explanation, what we would be doing for the child if we took him out of the theater — whose pictures he had always supposed to be magic-made — and showed him the camera, the studio, the actors and actresses, the stages and directors, scenarios, lighting effects — the mass of *natural* forces through whose application every picture is made.

We hope this lesson will do for you much more than that. We shall show you how certain every day, ever-operative *natural laws* are behind every individual drama; how everything in your life is made, directly or indirectly, consciously or unconsciously, *by you*, through your use or misuse of these same natural laws.

We are going to show you how your pictures are made — the machinery back of every movie you have ever put on in your own life; why you played the role you did and why you are playing, at this moment, the very part you are.

It is our sincere hope that you who read these pages will, from this day onward, apply these laws in your own life, for by so doing you shall attain your deepest and dearest desires.

A Law-Ruled World

We, like the babe at the movies, live in the delusion that things are only what they seem — a maelstrom in which we are caught, a moving mirage that whirls and swirls and carries us on against our will.

Science shows us that everything in the universe has a cause and that the same cause always and invariably brings the same results. Nothing "just happens." There are *no accidents*. All occurs in accordance with divine, unchanging law.

The world we live in today is exactly the same world the cave man dwelt in. But civilized man, *through a working knowledge of law*, has brought out of these unseen and hitherto undreamed-of forces the things that make life livable, beautiful, uplifting.

The cave man called the lightning a god of wrath and fell down in fear when his flashes illumined the sky. Civilized man, through a study and understanding of law, brings that same force to bear on his problems and with it lights the world, heats his home, travels around the globe and talks, without wires, from one end of the earth to the other.

In the last twenty years science has been discovering that human health and disease, human success and failure, human happiness and unhappiness — all the problems of human life — are equally controlled by law; that man is a part *of,* not a part *from* natural and divine law; that the laws of the mind, body and spirit of every individual are ever operating and are ever bringing to him, in exact accordance with these laws, the things that come out in his life.

The stars shine out across the wide-domed space.
Faring their fleeting journey night and day;
Each keeping to its measured time and place,
According to the law each must obey.

And stars and souls, rosebloom and planet, whirled,
Obey the wondrous law that makes the world.

By Elsie Lincoln Benedict and Ralph Paine Benedict

Conscious Wishes

Every man and woman has many conscious wishes. They are in the surface mind, the busy brain that handles the affairs of the moment and the events of the day.

You have a conscious wish to arrive at the office in time to look through your mail before the opening hour. You have another conscious wish to remember a fact, statement, the amount of that check you must write.

You have thousands of these conscious wishes during the course of a busy day. They pass into and out of your mind without much ado.

Conscious Standards

As a result of your training, education, environment, experience, type, personality and several other things, you have acquired certain *conscious standards* — of what you *ought* to do and be and accomplish; of what you owe the world, society and your fellow-man; of the right and square way to treat people; of honesty, justice, fair play; of how much and how well a man ought to work to get on in life; of how you ought to act under all conditions; of what you ought to acquire, achieve, accomplish; of the heights to which you ought to rise; the influence you ought to wield; the prestige you ought to have; the good name, fame or glory you ought to win.

In short, you have built into that conscious mind of yours whole sets of ironclad ideals which you aspire to live up to.

Whether you have lived up to them in the past has depended on just one thing which you had in those past years; whether you are living up to them now, and in what proportion, all depends on how much of that same thing you have today.

Whether you will in the coming years live up to these standards, achieve these things you consciously strive for, will depend upon

how much you understand, amend and utilize that same something. That thing which determines it all— which has actuated directly or indirectly every act of your life — is :

149

Your Supreme, Subconscious Wish

One of the most recent and revolutionizing discoveries of science is that every human being has, in addition to these temporary conscious wishes and conscious standards, *one wish which overtops all others, a wish which is often secret and sometimes submerged, but which saturates his subconscious mind.*

This wish is never for one specific thing nor does it deal with details. It is not for certain *things*, nor even for specific *people* in our lives, but for a *condition in life* — an environment, a kind of expression — the untrammelled satisfaction of a basic instinct! The achieving of a great ambition in some general direction — the attainment of a beautiful character, the acquirement of riches or the winning of an immortal name. And sometimes — in fact all too often — the secret supreme wish is for none of these uplifting things but for others of a far different nature.

Life Built Around the Wish

The second great discovery which is revolutionizing the science of psychology is that *every human being builds his life around his supreme subconscious wish.*

Some build their lives around the supreme wish consciously; others, unconsciously or subconsciously; but each is building every year, every day, every hour, directly or indirectly toward the gratification of his deepest desire.

The average individual has never heard of this urge at whose behest he lays practically every plan of his life. He is often unaware of this intense yearning which dictates the direction of his energies, predetermines the trend of activities characterizing every week of his life; which actuates the manifold expressions of himself and which prejudices, pulls and pushes him in directions serving its purpose.

But this does not alter the fact that it is there and that it wields an influence upon our lives which, in the end, makes or mars them.

The Weak Link

We often wonder why a promising man with brains, education, advantages, good looks and every possible chance makes such a mess of his life.

Especially do we wonder why this intelligent individual should make the *same kind* of mistakes over and over, permitting this one species of weakness to ruin his existence.

"He is so unusual in so many ways," we say. "Why can't he see that it is only this one thing that is wrecking his chances? Isn't it too bad that a fine young man like that, with such splendid qualities, should permit one little thing to destroy him!"

In every such case — and there are many of them — the individual's supreme subconscious wish is for something which the giving in to this weakness brings him.

One Woman's Wish

A woman who was well known as a writer of superior magazine articles was an outspoken radical.

She lived in a suffrage state so had a vote and cast it consistently for a radical ticket. She believed in birth control and declared that if she ever married she would not feel entitled to bring children into the world — not only because it was, as she was fully convinced, too cruel to give them a chance, but because her mother had died in an insane asylum and her father in a tuberculosis hospital.

She lived in Arizona herself as a result of of a prolonged siege of the disease which had taken away one lung, but which seemed now to be under control.

This woman had a most unusual mind. Her conversation was as interesting as a play, her writing was scintillating and extraordinarily clever. She was widely read, a deep student and a most convincing speaker on these very subjects upon which she held such radical views.

She finally married. Her husband did not care for children. But once every year for twelve years now she has presented him with a son or daughter, and once with both!

All her friends say, "What in the world has come over Agnes? What became of her convictions? "

The answer is not far to seek. Agnes, under all her conscious attitudes, had a deep, devouring, desperate desire.

Far back of and behind and beyond these surface things there was a supreme subconscious wish. That wish was to be the mother of a large family.

Reason, common sense, horse sense and her sense of justice told her that she — in whose veins ran two taints — had little right to jeopardize innocent lives.

Intelligence and human sympathy told her that life — never easy for the strongest — would be cruelly savage to the handicapped. Study and thought convinced her conscious mind that one hampered as she was might better be educating the world toward social and political betterment than adding to its population.

But the moment opportunity offered away went every conscious conviction, every standard of the years — and in came the subconscious urge! It took possession. Or rather, it *kept* possession. For it was the working out of that old subconscious longing which caused her to marry at all.

And this brings us to the third great new discovery:

You Get What You Want Most

This newest, hitherto unpublished and most far-reaching of all the discoveries concerning the laws of human life is that *every human being GETS his supreme subconscious wish.*

At first glance he may question this; but five minutes of honest self-inventory serves to convince every person that it is literally, *utterly true.*

You, for instance, may say, " That can't be true. Why, I wanted a college education more than I wanted anything else in the world. I have wanted it for years and I have failed to get it!"

You are sincere in saying this — just as you have been sincere all the time in telling the same thing to yourself and your friends.

But if you will look deep into your own heart you will find that at least one other desire — perhaps a dozen of them — takes precedence, in your secret list, of this desire for a college education.

You may never have stopped to think of it before (and the probabilities are you have said it so often you fully believe it) but when you come right down to it, there are several things you want more than you want that college education. Yes, I know, something was always happening to prevent your going to college. There always is something happening to prevent things, and it prevents them too — all but your *real wish!*

When things happen to that, you go right over them. You find a way out. You do *something* to counteract it. You invariably ride over the difficulty — and *do it!*

From Observation

During the past ten years at least a hundred men and women have told us "the only thing on earth they had wanted most was to go to college but it had been impossible."

What were the psychological facts?

One young man who vehemently denied at first that he had ever desired anything as much as a college education, finally said that he believed he wanted to get married more than he wanted an education. This was the reason for his marrying instead of going to college.

Another who was certain that nothing had ever superseded his desire to go to college realized that what he had really wanted most was to travel. He hoped to go abroad and had decided a college education would help to give him a keener appreciation of the things he expected to see in his travels.

When he was given a position which took him several times a year to London and Paris, he subconsciously gave up the college idea, though continuing consciously to think and to declare that it was a great disappointment.

These are not deliberate deceptions we practice upon ourselves and our friends. We know very little about our real selves until we study the human sciences. The result is that only an occasional individual ever meets the stranger that lives in his skin!

What You Really Want

A man once said to us, "I cannot believe that every person gets his supreme, subconscious wish. I have loved a woman for eight years. My subconscious wish was to have her. I haven't gotten her, and what is more, it doesn't look as though I ever would. Yet I have tried with all my might to win her."

We explained to him this other great law:

Our supreme subconscious wish is never for any specific thing or person but for a condition, a certain avenue of self-expression.

The supreme wish saturates the subconscious mind but the subconscious mind never knows nor cares anything about details nor the fine points concerned with methods. All it knows is overwhelming desire for a certain kind of *satisfaction for your personality as a whole.*

The conscious mind supplies methods, means, the vehicles for realizing these subconscious desires.

Your Special Train

These two great minds of ours may be likened to the equipment of a freight train. The subconscious mind supplies the steam, the *going power*, the *forces* necessary to your arriving at a certain destination.

It is unlike steam in this, however: it knows the *general direction* in which you want to go and is concentrated on your getting there. But it allows the engineer (your conscious mind) to select the crew, the paraphernalia for the journey and to take whichever one of the tracks it prefers.

But it gives you no peace save when you are traveling in the general direction of its {and your) subconscious aim!

It stays out of sight, but goads, drives and lashes you whenever you start down a sidetrack — and gives you its full help only when you get back on the main line.

What He Really Wanted

What this man really wanted was not this, nor any *one specific* woman, but some general kind of *self-expression* for his personality which he considered the possession of her would make possible for him. In other words, she was what every individual is to the subconscious mind of his lover — the *means to an end*

No adult man or woman lives who subconsciously loves another man or woman. The subconscious knows no individuals *as such.* It is not concerned with the personnel of anything — only with *results.*

Your subconscious knows no one but *you.* It has no desire, no religion, no aim, no interest save the accomplishment of *your wants. You* are its world, its master, its adored. The result of the universe is, to your subconscious mind, only a place in which you function, a stage on which you *act,* the world in which you *live* and move and have your being.

Self and the Subconscious

"Where do I come in? " is the first question your mind puts to everything you ever hear, everything that is broached to you, everything that comes within the range of your consciousness.

If you cannot see wherein *you* are going to get self-expression of some sort you stay away from it. Even our most generous acts are performed more for our own self-expression than for the persons for whom we do them.

The man who gives his money to the poor and dies penniless has not really sacrificed himself. His supreme subconscious desire was for *that kind* of self-expression. He was happiest that way and did it because he could find more happiness in that than in keeping it for himself.

In other words, he *bought,* with his money, the thing that appealed most to him, and though in so doing he proved himself a higher, finer nature than the average, and deserves our admiration and respect as a superman, he is not to be credited with self-sacrifice.

What we call self-sacrifice is always the sacrifice of something the individual wants for something he *wants more* — therefore is not self-sacrifice at all.

Supermen and Superwomen

The big thing we must not overlook in this new understanding is that *the individual who prefers to use his money* this way, who gets his *greatest happiness out of helping others is a highly evolved individual, far ahead of his time* — spiritual in the highest, finest sense, sympathetic, superhuman.

You need not regret that you can no longer credit him with self-sacrifice. This kind of human being is far more admirable than one who would reverse God's first law of self- preservation. We know it *is* God's law because He puts it into every living organism.

Your first *duty* is to *yourself* — to make yourself the highest, best, biggest and broadest being you can be; and the proof of this lies in every living thing in the universe.

You can never help humanity very much till you can walk alone. Your first duty therefore, to the world and to yourself, is to *learn to stand alone!* Don't lop and lean and loll on other people.

First, develop your own backbone. Then, as you go along, help everybody, inspire everybody, uplift everybody — and don't forget to *start!*

Don't make the mistake that thousands of well-meaning people have — of waiting till your own life is perfect before beginning to give others a lift.

"You will pass this way but once," so scatter real help as you travel, but keep your life-belt on! Keep your head up, your eyes open, your heart gentle — but *keep climbing!*

What Mark Twain Said

If you would like to see what a great thinker says about these real human motives read the book Mark Twain wrote and which he directed should not be published till five years after his death, "What Is Man?"

In it he shows you, in better words than we can, how every act of every human being is for " the contentment of his own spirit."

156

The Real Reason

What about the man who thought his supreme subconscious wish had been for the woman he had courted eight years and didn't get?

He loved her with the only force an adult loves with — his conscious mind. His supreme subconscious wish for this particular kind of self-expression which he consciously decided such a mate would give him.

Consciously, therefore, he loved her personally, individually, devotedly. His subconscious mind, which can love none other than the person to whom it belongs, had no interest in her save as she promised to gratify that supreme subconscious wish for this particular kind of self-expression.

That this was precisely the situation was proved recently, when this very man was married to another woman, much like the one he had wooed so long — and whom he now feels he loved more than he loved the first.

"I realize fully now," he said not long ago, " that my supreme subconscious wish has always been for the *kind of home-life* these women would make possible.' Any woman who gave evidence of fulfilling this wish would have gotten a proposal out of this man.

Why and Whom We Love

Though it is a startling, and to many a shocking fact, it is nevertheless true that the people we love are desired, not for themselves but for ourselves, and loved to the *extent that they, directly or indirectly, aid in our own self-expression.*

All of which proves again how the beloved ego in each of us makes or mars our world.

The child loves best the parent who most aids it in expressing itself. The man loves best those women who aid most in his self-expression. Women love best those men who aid them most in their self-expression.

Every unmated person is seeking, as we have seen, a lover who recapitulates the symbol of his first great love.

But such a one, even if found, will never bring him continued happiness unless he be, in addition to this symbol, of a biological type which automatically aids in the self- expression of his mate.

When a man finds a woman who recreates his love-symbol (or visa versa) he can love her instantaneously, but if her biological type is such that she cannot aid in his *continued* self-expression he will eventually tire of her. The more she obstructs his self-expression, the sooner will he tire.

If she not only refuses to yield herself as an aid to the expression of his type and subconscious wish, but insists upon changes in him which enable her to express her own, he will gradually grow to dislike her. If she keeps it up he will ultimately, subconsciously hate her, though she be the mother of his children!

Why People Do Not Marry

Whenever an individual goes through life without marrying it is not because he does not desire a mate, but because marriage with any of the people he has seen would, in his opinion, *interfere with his supreme subconscious wish.*

Every unmated person desires a mate, but if he desires something else more — that is, if the desire for a mate is not his supremest desire — he will not marry until he finds someone who he is convinced will *not interfere* with his supreme subconscious wish.

Why Others Marry

Many men and women mate with one who does not remind them of their subconscious love-symbol, and they marry knowing this.

Whenever this happens it is because the finding of a mate who shall repeat this love- symbol is *not* this person's supremest wish. He feels that the one he has chosen will aid in that supreme wish, whatever it may be, and strikes a compromise.

Since that supreme wish is for something which to him is more desirable than the possession of an ideal mate he sacrifices the lesser to the greater. You do the same thing in every decision of your life.

Why You Give Up Things

You want many things, but you always give up those you want less for those you want most. Thus, in the by-and-large of your life you do what you *want* to do; you get the things you *really want.*

If you are unsuccessful it is because there was one or many things you wanted more than you wanted success.

Look back over your life and you will say that in your life *as a whole* you have been doing those things which, *in general*, appealed to you more than the kinds of things you refused to do.

Perhaps you want money and yet are poor.

But no one ever had a supreme subconscious wish for *money.* The subconscious, as has been stated, knows nothing of things, details, or the concrete. It knows only certain fundamentals — those big, basic urges of your personality.

It knows many of these but takes it upon itself to fulfill in your life *the one* which, above all others, you want most. It has never heard of money and never can, for money, as money, is nothing but worthless chunks of metal and useless pieces of paper. Even your conscious mind, which does know and deals with money, does not want *money* but only the *self-expression which money would bring.*

Since the subconscious gets for you whatever you want most, if the thing you want most is of such a nature that you have *got* to have money to get it, your subconscious will find a way for you to make money.

It can find the means to any end you supremely, subconsciously demand. It will do so by keeping your eyes open for opportunities furthering this end.

It deals only with ultimates. Money, which has less intrinsic and ultimate value than almost anything with which we come in contact, is never in any man's supreme subconscious wish *as such.* It is not even in the supreme wish of the miser, but is desired and obtained by him wholly and solely *as a means to protection.* (The miser is always the result of a fixed fear — the fear of poverty — the product of a poverty-stricken childhood.)

But because the fear-attitude prevents great results in any direction, the miser, with all his skimping, never makes a great deal of money.

No self-made millionaire in the world ever cared for money *as money.* He had some kind of supreme subconscious wish requiring money for its full expression. It is precisely this which, every rich person will tell you, drove him to make money.

Once it is made very few very rich people care for money. They conserve it only in so far as its conservation serves that same original wish.

Fame Through Fortune

Here is a man whose supremest subconscious wish is for fame. His subconscious, which knows and remembers everything about him, contains the necessary elements and brings them to the surface as they are needed He has certain gifts, talents, abilities. He lacks certain others. The quickest and surest route to the materialization of his supreme wish is through these talents. His subconscious suggests these routes.

If these talents are superior he will rise to fame through them. The greater these talents the greater the urge to express them and the greater his ability to serve, entertain, amuse, or enlighten the world. In return, the world applauds him, gives him fame, pays him well — and his supreme wish is gratified.

People are always glad to pay for what they like. The public is always generous to the able man. Whether or not he cares very much about money he is glad to have the public's money purely as a proof that he has succeeded — that his ego has satisfied itself, proven to itself that it *can* do this thing.

Ambitious Americans

In America success is all too often measured by money. Since money is the great American standard, and since every ambitious individual desires to live up to the standards of his environment, the ambitious American is compelled to seek money.

Let a man with a message attempt to carry that message to the American public. Though it be the greatest message in the world,

160

that public will not ask " How much *good* does this man do? " It will not even ask " What is his message *about?*"

This public will ask but one question. That question will consist of six words: *"How much money does he make?"*

Though you produce the greatest thing that has yet been produced, the American public will have none of it nor you if you cannot make it pay financially.

In self-defense, therefore, any person who has a great message to give to America is compelled to make that message pay. He must have the confidence of the public, as does any man who aspires to help the world. It is inconceivable to the average American that you could have anything worth while unless you are making a financial success of your life.

Instead of railing at the one who makes a great deal of money, use that energy to reeducate the public if you are really in earnest.

If You Want Money

If you want money you must do what every person did who ever made money: *produce something the world wants and knows it wants.* The world is always willing and glad to pay for what it really wants.

But it is determined *not* to pay for what it does not want, just because you want or need the money. And you can't blame it, can you?

Remember, you can only get money via *the world.* For it you must give value received. To do that easiest and quickest, you must make your supreme subconscious wish into a real desire *to produce something the world needs.* Once you have done this, the same forces which have always and will forever bring your supreme wish to pass in your life will point the way.

Your Successful Subconscious

Let us repeat: Your supreme subconscious wish dictates your life. It permits nothing seriously to interfere with its materialization. It is autocratic, implacable. What you want *most of all*, as a *condition* in your life, it will get for you.

161

In the getting you are often compelled to forego many or hundreds of things you want, but want *less.*

Your subconscious causes you to sacrifice these many things, and all things, if necessary, to the accomplishment of this supremest desire.

You must relinquish this, sacrifice that, forego the other. You *feel* all this in the depths of you. You do not like giving up the eating of your cake but — if you want the *cake more* than you want the pleasure of eating it, you will *not* eat it. Your subconscious and supreme wish will not permit you to. You made this choice yourself. Your subconscious takes you at your word, and not only relieves you of most of the labor by performing it itself, but refuses to permit you to greatly interfere with its activities.

Your conscious mind may falter and fail, but your subconscious, once saturated with your supremest desire, is always successful.

Subconscious of the Successful

The most successful men and women, once they have decided on their supreme aim, automatically adapt themselves to this great law.

Every successful person that ever lived gave up many things for the sake of his big ambition. At first he did so consciously. He had many backslidings. But as time went on his conscious and subconscious minds worked in such unison that his subconscious sentinel learned at last habitually to turn away from the door of his mind the things that would interfere with the big desire, without his ever being conscious of making a decision.

This is the secret of the great concentration, the "one-pointed' mind, the keen thought- capacity of every successful person.

His mind is not necessarily superior to that of the average man, but he does what the average man fails to do — keeps the decks clear and ready for business. He keeps out of his mind, automatically, habitually, consciously and unconsciously the thieves that would steal his mental energy.

After a time his subconscious becomes so expert that it short-circuits most of the wasteful, inimical things that are headed for his mental house, thus conserving his mentality for the constructive, the worthwhile, the *big thing* in that man's life.

The subconscious performs, in addition to all its other services, the function of an expert private secretary guarding the front office of the mind. He permits no visitor to interrupt the president in his private office when he is at work.

Thus is the president (his conscious mind) enabled to think out the plans, the ways, means and methods for making him a success.

Your Wish is a Want

The reason your subconscious attains for you your supremest wish is that this deepest desire of your life is not a mere wish at all, but a goading, driving, overwhelming *want.*

It is necessary, up to this point, because of the inadequacy of language, to call this a wish. But from this moment onward we shall call it what it is — the supreme subconscious want. There is a world of difference between wishing and wanting.

When you wish for a thing you get it — sometimes. When you *want* a thing you *always* get it. For a want is not a mere surface feeling, but a deep, desperate craving that demands not things nor people, nor trifling details, but great general outlets of self-expression. You must satisfy the greatest one or die.

This supreme want is far more important than life itself to many human beings.

These are the supreme successes. They had rather die than miss their goal. The man who wants a thing more than he wants life is filled with an enthusiasm so irresistible that it literally burns away all obstacles from his pathway.

Why Are We Unhappy ?

If each of us is getting his supreme subconscious want why are so many of us unhappy? The answer is evident.

This supreme subconscious want in each of us is a primal, instinctive thing. It may be founded in high, recent and civilized instincts, and often is; but much more often the deepest desire of the average organism is for the gratification of a primitive, uncivilized instinct, urge or tendency.

163

These primitive instincts are out of place in the world of today. Our training is against them; our cultivated ideals are against them; society in general is against them. But the law of the supreme subconscious want is immutable.

If this primitive thing is what he really wants more than anything else in the world, the law brings it to pass in his life. If it is too far removed from modern instincts his family, his friends and the world will call him a coward, a ne'er-do-well, a beast or a criminal — depending upon the particular instinct which, out of the primitive group, is most over-developed in him.

All the while he will be wishing to live up to his higher instincts. He has many others of high order. One of these — and it exists in every human being — is the instinct of approbation.

He wishes the approval of his fellows; he wishes to do and be and have the things that make them like, admire, respect and follow him; but his supreme want must and *will* express itself. All its enemies must go by the board. He makes excuses, he equivocates, he apologizes, he tries to justify his failures to the world, whose opinion he so much values.

Most of all, he suffers.

But he feels that he suffers less than he would were he to give up his supremest want — so he pays the price.

Sympathy, Not Censure

How sad a sight is this suffering man — existing in the twentieth century but *living* in primitive ages!

What a contrast to that fortunate one whose supreme subconscious want is in harmony with modern standards, whose deepest desire happens to be toward the production of those things the world needs.

Give him the laurels he has won, but don't forget to give to the other the sympathy and understanding to which every unsuccessful soul is entitled.

Through this you may reach his feeling, subconscious mind, and once there you may, with patience and earnestness, help him to change the subconscious desire which has ruled and ruined his life.

How to Help Humanity

Parents, teachers, preachers — the whole world — may talk, argue, beseech, implore, preach to the weak of the desirability of better things, but you will never help him appreciably until you induce him to change his supreme subconscious desire.

The trouble with most of those who have tried to make men see the error of their ways was not lack of arguments, intellect, nor faithfulness. Thousands of high-minded men and women who earnestly desired to help others have had all these, and failed to understand the ineffectiveness of their efforts.

The explanation lies in human psychology. Reasons, arguments, facts and illustrations are things which appeal not to the subconscious, but to the conscious mind.

To change a man's supreme subconscious want from low to high, from weak to strong, from evil to good, you must reach *his subconscious mind.*

To reach any individual's subconscious mind you must talk the language of the subconscious, which is not thought but *feeling*.

As stated many times before in this course, the subconscious mind is not a thinking, intellectual mind, but a feeling, instinctive mind. It is not appealed to by reason but by "the spirit" of a thing. It is deaf to thoughts, but keenly alert to emotions.

You will never be able to help humanity rise to better things until you learn to deal with men and women from your heart to theirs.

The Spirit of Sincerity

This is the real explanation of the magic of sincerity. When a man is sincere, we do not so much think it as feel it. His heart is right, and our own communes with it. Words and phrases are weak, thin and pale beside that emotional certainty.

To convince, to inspire, to help another, to change his subconscious content, you must feel what you are saying. You must mean it. Your interest must be real. It must be genuine.

To Help Yourself

To help yourself you must do exactly the same thing in the same way and with the same feeling. You must think of yourself as two persons, which in reality you are: the weak self and the strong.

Put you strong self at the helm. Make up your mind that that strong self is going to dictate your life hereafter.

Treat your weaker self as though it were another individual — an individual whose faults threaten to ruin your life.

You are going to be fair to this individual, to recognize that he is the product of primitive ages and therefore not responsible for his weaknesses. But you are not going to allow him to wreck your twentieth-century life.

You must first *want* to help yourself. Then you must realize that you *can* remake your life. You must feel it, believe it, *know* it.

You want happiness, not mere gratification of an instinct; and it is happiness you must have to stay well, to achieve, to realize your best, to really *live.*

If your subconscious want clashes with your ideals you must and can change that subconscious want for a better one.

" Can it be done? " you say.

It *has,* and *is* being done every day by thousands of men and women whose instincts are just as out of date as yours.

You have a brain, a mind, a spirit. It is for you to decide whether you will live in the basement of your lower nature or in the sun parlors of your highest self.

All these instincts, including the one that has been ruining your life, are under the full control of your conscious mind at any moment you desire to use that power.

Until recent years science had not discovered what it was that was wrecking human lives, and only recently did we discover how to remedy it when we did know. It is only just *now* that we have discovered the laws given in this lesson whereby we can easily and quickly remake our lives. The greatest of all these discoveries is that you can:

Change Your Subconscious Want

You can change the content of your great subconscious mind and direct its forces toward the achievement of any goal you desire.

If you will have faith, patience, and even a little determination, you can drain out of it the things you do not wish to keep and fill its batteries with the positive power you need for the accomplishment of your highest aims.

To Change Your Subconscious Want

To change your subconscious want from evil to good, from destructive to constructive, you need only to use the shortest, surest, swiftest inlet by which anything enters your subconsciousness — your *conscious mind.*

The conscious mind is the president of your corporation. It has the brains and intelligence fitted to cope with modern life and your personal problems.

Your subconscious is but the great factory which carries out the president's orders. It is obedient to his will and his demands, exactly as the privates are obedient to the commander-in-chief of an army.

The average man, or woman, makes a failure of his life because he allows his conscious mind to abdicate, after which the mob in his primitive subconscious mutinies.

Stop wallowing in the trenches of your subconscious and take command of that army. Consciously decide what it is that your standards demand, and then apply the great laws to enforce your orders exactly as a general relies upon the laws of court-martial when necessary with his army.

Making Life a Masterpiece

After you have decided what your standards and ideals demand; after you have realized that you, like thousands of others, can get whatever you want, whenever that want becomes the supreme one in your subconscious mind, set about changing the old want for the new. You can do so by the very simple but stupendous law of suggestion.

That law is this: *Whatever your conscious mind affirms, visualizes and suggests to the subconscious, the subconscious will build into your life.*

Suggest to your own subconscious that this thing which you want you are *going to have*; that nothing shall prevent it; that it is already *coming true* in your life. Whenever a thought to the contrary enters your mind eject it, not by force, but by turning your attention to the *thing you want.*

Talk, walk, act, speak, and *think* as you believe that better self will when full grown.

Because the subconscious mind cannot resist repeated suggestions from you, it will begin to take on the new qualities. You will see some of its results within a day; more in a week, many in a month, and in a year will have so greatly altered your life, capacities, and powers that yours will be a new world.

Your new and strong subconscious want, becoming at last embedded in the subconscious, will, of its own force, *bring itself to pass* in your life *exactly as the old and outgrown desire once did.*

Thus will you attain your supreme wish; thus will you be happy; thus and thus only will you become good, and great, and gloriously strong. Thus you may and *shall* make of your life a masterpiece.

SO HERE THEN ENDETH "HOW TO UNLOCK YOUR SUBCONSCIOUS MIND THROUGH THE SCIENCE OF MENTAL ANALYSIS," THE SAME BEING AN EXPOSITION IN EVERY- DAY LANGUAGE OF THE FACTS AND FINDINGS OF PSYCHOANALYSIS, AND THEIR APPLICATION TO THE PROBLEMS OF EVERYDAY MEN AND WOMEN, BY ELSIE LINCOLN BENEDICT, FIRST LECTURER IN AMERICA TO PERSONALIZE AND POPULARIZE THESE LESSONS; ALSO BY RALPH PAINE BENEDICT, WHOSE KNOWLEDGE INSPIRED THE GIVING OF THE FIRST LECTURES AND THE WRITING OF THIS BOOK *» PRINTED AND MADE INTO A BOOK BY THE ROYCROFTERS AT THEIR SHOPS AT EAST AURORA, COUNTY OF ERIE, STATE OF NEW YORK, IN THE YEAR NINETEEN HUNDRED TWENTY-TWO

By Elsie Lincoln Benedict and Ralph Paine Benedict

Other Books of Interest:
Unleashing the Power of Your Subconscious Mind

All edited by: Pat Stephenson. To easily find the complete, and most up-to-date list of books edited by Pat Stephenson on this topic, do a search on Amazon under "books" and enter "Pam Stephenson" (with quotation marks).

The Great Within, by Christian D. Larson
Just Be Glad, by Christian D. Larson
The Mountain Trail and Its Message, by Albert W. Palmer
What is Worth While? By Anna Robertson Brown Lindsay

CPSIA information can be obtained at www.ICGtesting.com
Printed in the USA
BVOW08s0332040315

390118BV00013B/32/P